Doing Your Research Project in Sport

Chris Lynch

LearningMatters

First published in 2010 by Learning Matters Ltd

All rights reserved. No part of this publication may be reproduced, stored in a retrieval system, or transmitted in any form or by any means, electronic, mechanical, photocopying, recording, or otherwise, without prior permission in writing from Learning Matters.

© 2010 Chris Lynch

British Library Cataloguing in Publication Data

A CIP record for this book is available from the British Library

ISBN: 978 1 84445 164 7

This book is also available in the following ebook formats:

Adobe ebook ISBN: 978 1 84445 647 5

EPUB ebook ISBN: 978 1 84445 646 8

Kindle ebook ISBN: 978 1 84445 964 3

The right of Chris Lynch to be identified as the author of this Work has been asserted by him in accordance with the Copyright, Designs and Patents Act 1988.

Cover design by Toucan Design

Text design by Toucan Design

Project Management by Swales & Willis Ltd, Exeter, Devon

Typeset by Swales & Willis Ltd, Exeter, Devon

Printed and bound in Great Britain by TJ International Ltd, Padstow, Cornwall

Learning Matters Ltd

33 Southernhay East

Exeter EX1 1NX

Tel: 01392 215560

E-mail: info@learningmatters.co.uk

www.learningmatters.co.uk

Doing Your Research Project in Sport

Active Learning in Sport – titles in the series

To order, please contact our distributor: BEBC Distribution, Albion Close, Parkstone, Poole, BH 12 3LL. Telephone: 0845 230 9000, email: learningmatters@bebc.co.uk. You can find more information on each of these titles and our other learning resources at www.learningmatters.co.uk.

To my mom

Contents

Acknowledgements

Throughout this book I have emphasised how you should draw upon the resources of those around you – in particular, draw upon human resources to help in any way they can. In writing this book I have done exactly that. I have drawn upon the resources of many people and now that writing is complete I would like to sincerely thank them and acknowledge the help they have given me.

Some need to be thanked for their suggestions on the way the book could be improved. For example, the wisdom of 'just tell them to do a Google search' as well as insistence that the wise words of Fabio Capello and Voldemort appear at appropriate places within the text. You know who you are.

I would like to thank Jenn, who in her quiet way allowed me the space and time as well as the gentle encouragement to get the project finished, even when the words I was going to write got in the way of fun.

My biggest thanks go to Anthony Haynes. Since the moment we made contact and through a very long time he has been incredibly enthusiastic and positive about this book. He has also shown immense staying power as I procrastinated my way from chapter to chapter. I would also like to thank Learning Matters, who I am sure would have lost patience with me if it were not for the persistence of Anthony's reassurances that the book was coming.

Finally, I have to thank myself, a pat on my back for finally doing it . . . well done Lynchy!

Part 1

Getting to the start line

Chapter 1
Your research project and this book

Learning Objectives

This chapter will help you to be able to:

- use this book to make your research project a successful one;
- understand that this book and other resources are there to help you;
- make best use of your time when searching for information in this book.

You will also be able to:

- feel more confident that the research project will be a successful one.

Introduction

Welcome to the world of research in sport and exercise. Welcome also to the beginning of your research project. You should consider your research project a journey: by setting out on that journey you are about to join a community of people who are crucial in developing our understanding of the interesting and vast area that is called sport and exercise. The journey will bring huge gains in knowledge and understanding and will benefit you greatly in all you do from now on. The outcomes of your project may also provide some of the lifeblood on which those engaged in researching these fields depend. It is not a journey that you have to take alone and this book is here to help you as you go on your way.

This may be the first time you have had to carry out a research project, and you may not be very clear about what is involved in undertaking a project from conception to completion. This book is designed to help you understand what is involved in bringing a successful research project to completion and to guide you through the process – so take a deep breath and relax, help is at hand.

I assume that for many reading this book the research project is an integral part of an academic award. Therefore the project is likely to carry significant weight towards that award and it is best to get it right, first time. Using this book will help you in achieving that aim, but it is not the total solution. Research projects tend to follow similar processes and there is generally a common way in which they are structured. However, your awarding institution will have its own requirements and you must make sure that you are completely familiar with these. Your own institution will be the one, after all, who assesses the project. This book can act as a valuable generic resource but you do need to find out from your institution what is required of you in terms of word counts, submission dates, and project proposals, as well as many other aspects.

Wherever and however you are studying, there will be an abundance of help available to you if you look. It is likely you will have a supervisor or tutor specifically to look after you while you do your project. There will be people and resources available to help and advise on some of the trickier bits in carrying out a research project, such as the correct referencing style to use and how to write a report coherently. Research is a collective enterprise and it is likely you will have peers at your institution who are going through, or have already gone through, the same process and who can help. Make sure you make as full use of those resources as you do of this book. Ultimately, however, the success of this research project will depend on you.

How this book is structured to help you

I thought a sporting analogy would be the best way to illustrate how to approach a research project in sport and exercise, and so this book is split into three sections, each with a sporting theme to its title:

- *Getting to the start line*;
- *You're off*;
- *Crossing the finishing line*.

Getting to the start line is all about the preparation you need to do to ensure your project is a successful one. Like all sports people, the performance is only as good as the preparation and so time spent preparing is essential. You will notice that most of the book falls in this section. Through this preparation you will discover how to research your topic area and to develop your question, as well as how to design your method of data collection.

You're off will help you understand and deal with some of the practicalities of a research project. They include, amongst other things, gaining informed consent and considering the ethics of your project, writing the method, and analysis of the data.

Finally, *Crossing the finishing line* is there to help you ensure the finished report or research product is written well and all the relevant parts are brought together smoothly and logically.

Each chapter begins with Learning Objectives, such as those at the beginning of this chapter. They are there to help you understand what the chapter will help you with. Review them as you progress through the chapter to be clear on what you have learned and understood. Once you are fully familiar with the chapter, you can check your knowledge and understanding against them.

This book is specifically designed to help you conduct your research *project*. It is designed as a practical resource to accompany you during your project. Think of it as a 'guide-by-your-side'. As such, this book differs from general research methods texts. Such texts provide a grounding in research methods in general because an education in research methods is educationally valuable in its own right and because modules on research methods are often intended to provide the foundation on which you, when it comes to conducting a *project*, will then build.

Of course, there is some overlap between general research methods texts and this book. It would hardly be possible to write a guide to research projects without saying something about research methods in general. This book, however, does not seek to provide a comprehensive introduction to research methods in sport and exercise. There are other good texts around already that do that (an example of which is

Research Methods in Sport by Mark Smith, also published by Learning Matters). Rather, *this* book focuses on the execution of research in the context of your project. The material provided here on research methods in general, therefore, provides a refresher course, designed to remind you of key points concerning research methods and to direct you to further resources for more comprehensive or detailed treatment.

On many courses, you study a module on research methods well before – perhaps even a year before – embarking on a research project. Think of a book such as Mark's as the one you need for the former, and this one as your companion for the project.

Throughout each chapter there will be plenty of activities, tips, hints and checklists to help with your understanding, as well as guides towards further reading. There will also be real comments from those whose experience you can draw on when carrying out your research project.

It is always good practice to come back from time to time to review different chapters as the research project develops, to help with those little sticking points that undertaking any research project will always throw up. Above all, remember a project is not there to stress you out, it's there to help you learn and understand, and you can make it fun.

Enjoy it – and here's to completing a successful project in sport.

Chapter 2
Getting to the start line:
the basis of research

Learning Objectives

This chapter will help you to be able to:

- understand the need for research in sport and exercise;
- see opportunities where you can apply your understanding for the research process to potential projects;
- understand the necessary characteristics of a researcher.

You will also be able to:

- define what research is.

Introduction

You need to read this chapter as it gives an essential overview of the why and how of sport and exercise research to anyone who is about to undertake a research project for the first time. The information you will find here will introduce and underpin the ideas and understanding you need in order to complete a successful research project.

By undertaking a research project, you are about to start to develop research skills and gain a deeper understanding of a given topic or area in sport and exercise. The work you will do in this project will require you to work more independently than before and so understanding some of the skills and characteristics of a researcher is vital. From learning about the skills and characteristics of a researcher you will be able to reflect upon your own skills and characteristics and develop yourself further. You will gather information from various sources, and need to be able to read, interpret and critically evaluate this information in more depth than you may have done previously. A research project is generally considered a culmination of your learning, and it is best to support that learning through understanding the basis of what research is, and what a researcher is.

To understand the process you are about to embark upon, you will need some understanding of what the basis of research is, and the research context of your specific project. The first thing we need to establish is what exactly research is and what need there is for it. So we begin this chapter by examining the need for research, both how that need is driven scientifically and also how it contributes academically to the pursuit of your award.

The chapter then moves on to the basics of research. This begins with an examination of the different purposes of research, before a discussion of the process that research follows. Understanding that process is vital to help you ensure that your project keeps moving at the pace required. Next, we will look at you as a researcher, and examine the qualities you will need to have or to develop in order to be successful as a researcher.

What exactly is research?

This is a question that is always asked by lecturers and tutors; you may well have already been asked it in a research methods class or lecture. Often the answer is that it is about gathering information, trying to answer questions, finding solutions to problems, or something similar to this. This is true, and it is natural that this is your answer because when you have had to research in the past, to write essays or answer a question, that is probably what you have done. These answers can and should be built upon in order to understand what research in sport and exercise is. When we consider the question what *exactly* research is, we need to consider how we go about researching, the actual processes involved. We also need to think of the definition in the context of a research project, not as an answer to an essay question. We need to add a few more things to make our definition of research more complete.

Whenever we carry out a research project, it is vital that we have a planned system behind our method of gathering information. A planned system ensures we are thorough, collecting everything we think we need to answer the question we have; we need to try to think about every eventuality that can influence our data collection and plan for this too. Considering the level of planning that is needed we could define research as a systematic process of discovery and advancement of human knowledge (Gratton and Jones, 2003, p4).

We could go further than just the planning side when we think of defining research in the context of a research project. There is also the process you go through when collecting information and then reporting it back. We can define research as the planned and systematic collection, analysis, and interpretation of data. A definition that tutors and lecturers may welcome is that research is the process of applying creative thinking in a logical way to the acquisition and creation of knowledge informed by theory and practice and informing theory and practice.

The definition we now have for research has progressed a long way from where we started. Read it again, breaking it down into the distinct different parts. You will see research is the process of applying creative thinking in a logical way. A research project can be creative and you can think creatively but also in a logical way. The acquisition and creation of knowledge is essentially what research is all about. You are not only acquiring knowledge, gaining knowledge, but perhaps your research might create some new knowledge that can contribute to that lifeblood of sport and exercise we talked about in Chapter 1.

The knowledge you gain or create should always be informed by both theory and practice. It must have an evidence base that has been correctly applied. Equally the knowledge you gain and create can inform theory and practice. Your research can form part of that evidence base for others to base their theory and practice. Now thinking of research in those terms should get you excited about undertaking your research project.

For inspiration, and to build my confidence, I like to read this quotation from the Nobel Prize-winning scientist Julius Axelrod.

I soon learned that it did not require a great brain to do original research. One must be highly motivated, exercise good judgment, have intelligence, imagination, determination, and a little luck. One of the most important qualities in doing research, I found, was to ask the right questions at the right time.

The need for research

Because you are most probably doing a research project as part of an academic award at an awarding institution, you may be asking yourself why you are required to do a research project at all. How will doing a research project benefit you? The answer to this question is very broad but part of the answer is in the approach a research project requires. It is very different to the academic subjects you have already studied because you will have to work more independently than before. You will also develop a whole range of skills that you may never have used before. Your tutors and lecturers know that innumerable organisations and agencies need personnel that have these skills and the ability to work independently. So whether a student, an employed professional or someone engaged in voluntary work with an organisation, understanding, researching and doing a research project gives vital skills for employment and life. This does not answer the big question though, which is: what need is there for research?

I am a natural consumer of research. This is because I am an academic and so it is important that I am aware of current developments that are discovered through ongoing research. I know that much of the material I use in my teaching is commonly accepted, but it is only accepted because it is knowledge that has enough evidence to back it up. In other words, the concepts and ideas that I teach are grounded in theory and practice. They have been researched thoroughly and the weight of evidence suggests that what I teach is true. That is not to say that this does not change. It does as research gathers more evidence, new ideas can and do develop, existing ideas are challenged.

As a tutor I often get inquisitive students who ask the most thought-provoking and sometimes awkward questions, and very occasionally I cannot answer them! (This happens *very* occasionally, I might add.) As an educator it just would not do to say *I don't know*; it is better to say, *if I don't know, I am going to find out and so should you, so we can chat about it next week*. I say this because it is likely that the question they ask has been researched in some way and some evidence exists that could answer the question, at least in part. If, after looking thoroughly, no evidence seems to exist, then the question that has been asked is worthy of research and could be a worthwhile research project.

Learning Activity 2.1

Having questions in your mind is the best way to initiate your own research question for your project. It is this simple starting point of enquiry that can sow the seed from which a research project can develop.

- Do you have questions about topics already? Can you think of more?

Write them down, perhaps in a journal or research notebook and see if they can be developed further. It is good practice to record ideas; even if they are not used right now, who knows what the future may bring? One of these questions could be the starting point for your research project.

Of course, one of the great things about working in a community of researchers is that other researchers will not take the research you present as being fact: they will explore it themselves and approach it with a critical eye. Why is this a great thing to do, you ask? It is great because the evidence generated needs to be confirmed as being correct. Good research should always be repeatable. Even now, as I read research articles and books I find challenges to commonly accepted ideas. As a researcher this is very comforting, because it is vital that through research we still challenge existing ideas as well as generating new knowledge. The result is that our knowledge and development will continue to grow on a grounded evidence base. For your research project, you may consider carrying out research that examines an existing idea or concept instead of looking for something not already researched. In research having a critical eye on what has been found in the past is as important as having an inquisitive and curious thought about the present and future. There is a definite need for research, if we are to feel confident about the things we assume to be true.

Of course, existing research is an essential resource for your own research project. Chapters 3 and 4 look at how to search and use the literature to develop a question, but what we should be asking at this stage is, what have other studies found about topics you are interested in? It is important to know what the current state of knowledge is. Try and look at as much recent research around topics of interest to you as possible. You are using research to establish whether you are about to research something which has been studied extensively before, or whether you are finding a gap in the existing knowledge. If you are about to research something that has already been extensively studied, what are you adding to this? Are you trying to disprove existing theory? If so, where does your evidence come from that this may be likely? If you have found a gap in the knowledge, why have other researchers not spotted this before? Is it a topic worthy of research?

With all these questions, it is important to remember that if you are undertaking a research project for the first time, the tutors and lecturers are more likely to judge your success not on whether you are finding startling new evidence about an existing area or identifying a gap in existing knowledge but more on how you have approached and have gone through the processes of research. This book is about the process. It is not a research methods book but a practical guide.

The purpose of research

All research should be carried out with a specific purpose in mind and this purpose will influence how the research project is approached in its design. The purpose of research can be:

- exploratory;
- speculative;
- descriptive;
- explanatory;
- predictive; and/or
- evaluative.

Exploratory research

The purpose of exploratory research is to investigate an area or issue on which little previous work has been carried out. An organisation may use this type of research to discover whether or not a problem exists within it. In sport and exercise problems are generally clearly identifiable and so research with a descriptive purpose is used more than research with an exploratory purpose to demonstrate the degree of the problem, but that does not mean you should exclude exploratory research. You may know of an organisation or have tutors or lecturers that would like some exploratory research carried out on their behalf.

Speculative research

Sometimes research is implemented strategically, where researchers take account of current situations and speculate as to their future implications. For example, the introduction of a specific government policy might raise implications for practitioners involved in its implementation. Research of this nature might speculate as to what these implications might be, and develop a programme of inquiry that can inform future responses to these issues. Research with this purpose does occur in health settings within the field of sport and exercise. It tends to be funded as part of a larger project and may not be suitable for an academic project.

Descriptive research

Research that has a descriptive purpose aims to gather information that illuminates relationships, patterns and links between variables. A lot of research in sport and exercise has a descriptive purpose, and often forms the starting point for further investigations and further research with an explanatory purpose to help explain the mechanisms of what has been found. An example of a descriptive research project would be an investigation of the degree of dehydration in sports played during the summer months. An explanatory research project could then identify the mechanisms for dehydration in a particular sport; a study of this type could then also lead to a project that uses an intervention to counter the findings – this would be a research project with a predictive purpose.

Explanatory research

Explanatory research aims to show why relationships, patterns and links occur. Using the example from descriptive research, what is the degree of dehydration in sports played during the summer? Assuming a performance decline with dehydration was described, an explanatory research project could look at explaining the mechanisms by which performance declines in sports where dehydration occurs. This could only be approached of course once it is known that dehydration does occur, hence the initial need for research with a descriptive purpose.

Predictive research

The purpose of this type of research is to develop a model that predicts the likely course of events, given particular intervening variables or circumstances. Research with this purpose is used a lot in sport and exercise, particularly in experimental research, where a certain intervention is predicted to have a certain effect. An example may be that caffeine could improve reaction times. A researcher will set out a research project with a predictive purpose, hypothesising that caffeine will improve reaction times, and measuring one group against another.

Evaluative research

The purpose of evaluative research is to examine the impact of something, for example a new policy, event, law, or treatment regime, or the introduction of a new system. Again, research with this purpose is used a lot in sport and exercise, but usually towards the end of a series of research with other purposes.

So research can have many purposes, and often research with one purpose will lead on to research with another purpose. For example a larger-scale research project will often have smaller projects within it, one to describe what is happening, one to explore the mechanisms of what is happening, one to predict the effect of an intervention on what is happening, and perhaps one to evaluate on a longer-term basis the results of the intervention. Your tutors or lecturers may be involved in large-scale projects that have smaller projects within them. Chat to them and they may be able to give you some ideas for your own.

The research process

As we will see later in this chapter, golden rule number four of a successful research project is having a plan. To be able to plan properly you must have an understanding of the process that you are about to go through. If this is your first research project, then understanding the process of a research project is vital. Think of it as understanding the bigger picture, so that you can plan to take the smaller steps towards achieving the bigger goal. Researching and undertaking a research project is actually an enjoyable and very rewarding process, something that, when done correctly, can add to the knowledge and understanding of the world as we know it. It can also weigh you down unless you break it down into manageable steps. It can also be a very frustrating, time-consuming and mind-boggling thing so let us try and make things simpler, and see the process as a whole.

Consider the research process as a blueprint that will take you through from start to finish with the minimum of fuss and the maximum result. Please do not misunderstand: knowing how the process works will not reduce the amount of work you have to do to be successful, but what it will do is give maximum return from the work you put in. You will be working smarter. There are four key requirements to understanding and working with this blueprint.

1   You will have a question or problem. It may be that you are given the specific question or problem, or guided towards a particular area or left to your own devices to arrive at such a problem. Chapter 3 will help you develop a problem.
2   You will have to sift through a lot of data, research and reading, not only about the question or problem you have, but also about the best way to answer or solve it. This will require a lot of work, but doing the preparation really is worth it in the end.
3   You will need a valid and reliable method that you can use to answer your question or solve the problem. Chapters 5 and 6, *Designing an experiment* and *Non-experimental research*, will help you develop this.
4   You will need to reflect on points 1, 2 and 3 and discuss how the research you have carried out generates new knowledge or contributes or clarifies existing work. The second and third sections, *You're off* and *Crossing the finishing line*, will help you with this.

Now that we have examined the four key requirements to understanding and working with this blueprint, it seems like we have the beginning of a plan.

Case Study

Andy, a student who has recently finished a research project that examined the bio-mechanics of climbing techniques, commented:

When I started my project I had so many specific questions, like how many words, how should it be presented and so on. I quickly realised these questions were easy to find the answer to. What I really needed to know was how my project would develop … I needed to see the future!

The point Andy highlights here is that it is easy to find the answer to the specific questions but more importantly understanding how the overall process will develop will let you know when you need to ask and find the answer to those questions.

Familiarisation with the process of undertaking a research project in sport and exercise science is crucial to its success. The more familiar you become with what you are required to do generally, the easier and quicker you will be able to do the specifics, because you will understand how they fit in to the bigger picture.

Remember you are not the first to go through this process. It is likely that your institution has past research projects that you can look at. These will start to make the specific questions in your mind a little clearer. (How much writing will I have to do? How big is the literature review? What is presented in the results section?) There is also likely to be a guide produced by your institution or supervisor as to what is explicitly required. Start to go over these resources as early as possible and use them to help with your planning but do not get caught up in the fine detail just yet.

It is important to remember that you must conform to your institution's explicit requirements.

Learning Activity 2.2

Use the questions listed below to start to sketch out some of the requirements of your project. Write your answers in a journal used specifically for your project.

- Do you know what form your final research project can/must take? For example, is it a report, a dissertation or a poster?
- What type of research can/must you do? Must it be quantitative or qualitative, or can you use a mixed-method design?
- What is the word limit? Is there a guide to how far above or below you can go?
- What are the timescales you must follow? Can you start to break down the project into chunks? Does a proposal have to be submitted by a certain date?
- When is the final deadline?
- How will the project be assessed? What are the specific criteria for success?
- Do you have to do a research proposal?
- Who is your supervisor?

- What are the supervisory arrangements? How often can you see your supervisor, how do you get access to them, what help can they give you?
- In what form must the research be presented? Is it a written report, presentation, oral exam?
- What are the conventions that your institution requires you to follow? What is the required layout of the report, the report project binding, and style of referencing or academic style? Is there a guide?

Consider the four key requirements to understanding the research process that we highlighted earlier. You need a question; you will sort through a lot of information and previous research to inform the actions you take; you will develop from that a valid and reliable method to answer your question; and finally you report back the information you find. It is possible to put this into a model that will be really useful to follow so you are able to monitor your progress as well as see the bigger overall picture.

There have been a number of conceptual models that have been proposed that describe the research process. The model by Rummel and Ballaine is excellent as a basis for an overview as well as a guide as to where you are in the process. Shown in diagrammatic form, their model can be seen in Figure 2.1 (Rummel, 1963).

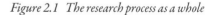
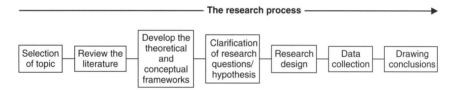

Figure 2.1 The research process as a whole

This model links very well with the four key requirements of research I highlighted earlier. It is clear to see the first two requirements within the first four stages of this model. The third requirement fits nicely into stages four, five and six and the final requirement, reflection, links to stage seven.

You could just as easily split the model into two phases. The first four stages are the planning phase and the final three are the realisation phase. So a research project is 70 per cent planning and preparation and 30 per cent data collection. This is interesting to remember because naturally when someone says 'a research project' you tend to think of lots of practical work and collecting data. That practical work is underpinned by a lot more preparation and planning than actual doing, however.

In planning, and as you progress through the project, you will feel you may have progressed a stage but then find it necessary to go back to an earlier stage before proceeding further. This is natural and occurs in many projects, so work with that and think of it as polishing everything you do. A word of caution is important here: it is likely your research has a time constraint and you do have to move onto the realisation stage with enough time to complete the whole project on time. Do not underestimate the amount of time it will take to actually collect the data. As you progress through the stages from beginning to end, each step should be viewed as being less reversible but not completely irreversible.

The model is a good way to monitor your progress, so we shall use it at the beginning of most chapters to show where you should be when considering that specific chapter.

> ## Reflection Point
>
> Richard is a student who attempted a research project in his final year but had to defer it as he attempted to balance his work commitments and his course requirements.
>
> *I did not start my project as early as I should have done. When I did start it, I realise now, I should have spent much more time in the planning and preparation stage. I found that I was trying to patch it up when a more solid foundation would have made a much better and easier to complete project. I did not make the same mistake second time around.*
>
> The point Richard highlights here is that it is easy to find the answer to the specific questions but more importantly understanding how the overall process will develop will let you know when you need to find the answer to those questions. He finished his project the following year.

Something that is often seen with those doing a research project for the first time is a realisation late in the project that perhaps the initial idea and the actual research needed to complete the work is not sustainable or achievable. This must be avoided as it results in a lot of time wasted. The best advice here is prepare, prepare, prepare. Also consult your supervisor as often as possible and seek their guidance.

The golden rules of a successful research project

As in all things we do there are some golden rules that should be followed. These really are golden rules because experience has shown that, especially for those undertaking research projects for the first time, the more they remember the golden rules, the more likely the project will be a successful one.

1 *Keep it simple.* For your research project to be successful it needs to be kept simple. That way you can give it the focus and the resources it needs without undue pressure to yourself and others around you. It does not have to be complex to be a successful and worthwhile project. When it feels as if it is becoming too complex or big, ask others to help you simplify and focus it with you.
2 *Don't try and do too much.* Following on from golden rule number one, do not try and do too much. You may be enthusiastic, you may have an enthusiastic supervisor, but you must be realistic about the scale and scope of what you can do within the time available to you and the available resources you can draw upon.
3 *Patience.* They say it's a virtue and nowhere is that more true when carrying out a research project. Every stage and step in the process will require you to make choices and decisions; be patient and make the best choices you can; do not be tempted to take short cuts.

4   *Planning is crucial.* If you plan each step and take those steps, reassessing your plan regularly, you will achieve a project to the highest standard you are capable of.

You as a researcher

So far in this chapter we have looked at the need for research and how the research process works. We need to now examine *you* as a researcher. The simple act of doing a research project means you are entering a community. It is a community of professionals who have developed expertise in similar areas and they will welcome you, but you have a responsibility to yourself and them when you join that community. That responsibility is to, as much as possible, ensure you have:

- open-mindedness;
- knowledge of a specific subject;
- intellectual curiosity;
- perseverance;
- honesty.

These are all important characteristics of a researcher and these are the reasons why.

Open-mindedness

A researcher should always keep an open mind to all possible options in deciding the questions to ask, the methods to use, and the possible explanations for results that occur. Always having a mind open to the possibility that there is another reason why something happens will help ensure that you do not limit your thinking.

Knowledge of a specific subject

A researcher will have an in-depth knowledge of a specific subject. When choosing the topic for your research, you should choose a topic that you enjoy, a stimulating area, or an area that interests you. By doing this you will inevitably have some knowledge of that specific subject. This needs to be deepened as the research progresses. You should start to search for the problems or controversies that exist. What problems have limited the study of the topic previously? Are there limitations that affect methodology?

Intellectual curiosity

It is very difficult to research a topic that you have no intellectual curiosity about. The stronger the curiosity, the more likely you are to read and learn about it. As the knowledge is gained, the intellectually curious want to know more. This is one of the reasons why a lot of tutors or lecturers at your institution will have a specialist area. They will have answered questions through their research in this area and as they do, more questions are raised and curiosity leads to more questions being asked.

Perseverance

Carrying out a research project is a very personal journey. It is a journey that travels from taking a single idea or aspect of interest all the way through to submitting the final report. Along that road you will need to read, think, analyse, interpret and write. To do this to the best of your ability certainly takes perseverance.

Honesty

It is vital that you are honest. There are temptations caused by a number of pressures, such as looming deadlines and the need to hand work in to be assessed. However, a researcher must always be honest with their sources of data, the amount of data they have and how they deal with it.

An important point to note here is that, with research projects and the pressures you may feel at times, there are no right or wrong answers, only answers to questions and explanations as to why things work or do not work as expected. Always remember this. Do not feel your research has to find something significant to be right; finding out that something is not significant is equally important.

Those are some of the key characteristics of a researcher; there are other things you could consider as attributes you will want to develop that you may or may not do now.

At times carrying out a research project can be a very lonely business, particularly when it seems all those around you are preoccupied with their own projects and have little time to help you. The ability to do some of the things listed here can help enormously.

- Talk to your peers. You will find many like-minded souls amongst your group of peers. There may be specific seminars or study groups that you can join in and chat with, but more likely are the others in your group who are carrying out similar work. Chat, share experiences, offer and receive supportive criticism, keep it positive. In an academic sense, this type of activity may seem a little foreign to you at this point, but seasoned researchers will do this a lot. Remember all you are doing is using the knowledge and experience of others in helping you interpret your own work and offering the same to others. This is much more like a professional researcher and less like a student.
- Accept useful criticisms. This can be difficult. You are working hard, fully involved in your research and the supervisor or a friend may offer a tough observation, give a critical reaction or ask an awkward question. This is only done because you both share a desire to make your research project as successful as it can be. In the early stages of research this is a really important thing to do, as it is essential that your research is sharp and focused. Later on some comments may not appear helpful, often coming a little too late to help. These are useful if you consider them as ways to improve if it were to be repeated. These reflections can then be noted in your discussion of the final project. A useful saying I found to help me when others offer advice is *always listen to advice, always act on good advice.*
- Be realistic and clear about the resources needed. When we talk of resources we talk not only of physical resources such as labs and equipment, but also of personal resources. Can you devote enough time to the project? Is what you want to do going to compromise ethical standards? Does it need expensive equipment to be successful?

- Keep an open mind on your project plan. It has been highlighted earlier that an essential characteristic of a researcher is an open mind. It is important in the early stages of planning that you do not commit yourself to the nature, shape and purpose of your project before you have even begun. To have an idea is excellent, much better than not having one, but have some flexibility in your thinking. You do need a research topic though, so do not ignore that.
- Stick to the requirements of your course or award. Whilst this book attempts to guide and see you through the process, it is the specific requirements of your institution that will determine the ultimate success of your project. Always make sure you produce work that meets these requirements. If in doubt always ask your tutor, lecturer or supervisor.
- Keep your friends close, but your favourite text books closer. In such a varied and wide ranging undertaking as a research project in sport and exercise you will need the help of many texts, articles and journals. At the end of the project your favourite texts should be close friends.
- Have a (flexible) timetable. You should base your project on a realistic but yet flexible timetable. A timetable helps keep a structure to a process – imagine how many lectures you would attend if you were not sure when they would be, or how long they would last, or for how many weeks they would run. Remember it will not only be your time that you are planning, you are considering the time that it takes to go through the processes, such as gaining permission to actually carry out your project or recruiting your participants to the study.

General requirements

It is always a good idea to review how things are going before you progress any further, so before we finish this chapter it is best to ask some questions that you should review and answer. Place yourself in the position of your project supervisor – if the answer you give is not what your supervisor would expect, it is a sign to you that you need to take some action on that point before going any further.

- Have you secured a supervisor for your research project?
- Are you starting to think about topics for your research project?
- Do you have a plan about what you need to complete a research project?
- Are you aware of what the main elements of a research project are?
- Do you think you have the skills to carry out a research project?
- If not, is there someone or something that can help you develop these skills that you lack?
- Do you understand what is meant by academic writing style?
- Are you clear about what plagiarism is?

Chapter Review

The take-home messages from this chapter should be:

- We can define research as the planned and systematic collection, analysis, and interpretation of data. We can apply creative thinking in a logical way to the acquisition and creation of knowledge informed by theory and practice and informing theory and practice.

- There is a need for research to inform both theory and practice and we use methods of research with specific purposes to carry out that research. The purposes of research can be exploratory, speculative, descriptive, explanatory, predictive, or evaluative.
- Understanding the research process – where you begin with a question or problem, sift through a lot of data, research and reading, develop a valid and reliable method and then reflect upon the process and findings – will help you break a major project down into manageable chunks. Using the four golden rules will also help in keeping the project on track.
- Be aware of the characteristics of a researcher. They may be characteristics you already possess or they may be ones you need to develop but try to keep an open mind, develop knowledge of a specific subject, maintain intellectual curiosity and, above all, persevere.

Further Reading

Gratton, C and Jones, I (2003) *Research Methods for Sport Studies*. London: Routledge.

Chapters 1, 2 and 3 of this text are excellent accompaniments to the material that has been presented here and offer specific sporting application that will help understanding.

Grix, J (2004) *The Foundations of Research*. Basingstoke: Palgrave Macmillan.

This is a very informative text that will help you to understand the basis and philosophy of research in a very general and broad sense.

Davies, MB (2007) *Doing a Successful Research Project*. Basingstoke: Palgrave Macmillan.

The first three chapters of this text will help to reinforce the need to plan and prepare to do a successful research project.

Chapter 3
Identifying problems and developing the research question

This chapter will help you to be able to:

- identify a research area and topic for investigation;
- focus your topic into a research question;
- understand how to put together a research proposal.

You will also be able to:

- write a first draft of your research proposal.

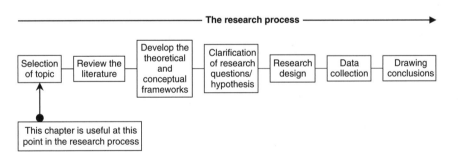

Figure 3.1 The research process: identifying problems and developing the research question

Introduction

This chapter is here to help you to turn the initial ideas you have about the research project that you want to do into the specific, technical statement of a research problem. This statement will subsequently provide an overall blueprint for your research project. It is important to recognise that this chapter provides help in an incredibly important and foundational aspect of your research project. Your success in carrying out your research project will be measured in terms of how well you have met the objectives you set for it at this stage. This is the time when you really have to get your thoughts in a logical and coherent order and decide exactly what it is you are researching. From the work completed now all else will follow: you are laying the foundation for your project.

The key to a successful research project is to have a well-defined problem to investigate in the first place. This problem-defining stage is a difficult stage when you are starting with a blank sheet of paper and are expected to produce a precise statement of work that is going to engage you for several weeks or months or even longer. It would actually be a lot easier to write such a specific description of your research when you have finished it – you will have a much clearer idea of exactly what your research involved once you have done it. Inevitably, and in some senses unfortunately, it is at the outset, when you are still a relatively inexperienced researcher, that you have to make firm decisions about a project that will change and develop as you learn new skills and knowledge. Spend a lot of time using this chapter; there will be many steps forward and quite a few back during this phase, but all of these steps will contribute to the success of the research project.

This chapter will begin by looking at how to define your problem by logically working through from how to choose a topic to actually defining the research question. There will be plenty of tips to help you, if you find this a hard process to work through. You will then set some research objectives and consider your research approach before finally drafting a research proposal.

Defining your problem

Identifying and then defining a problem to actually research is critical and is the first step to the success of a research project. So do not underestimate how important this task is. I am sure you will not and I am also sure you are thinking, but where do I begin? I can help answer that question, if we go back to the definitions of research in Chapter 2 and remember that research is a creative and logical process. Understanding this can help when trying to define the problem. We have to apply some of that creativity in a logical way and identify a potential problem to explore as a research project.

Begin by choosing a topic area

It is both an exciting and daunting prospect being given the task of carrying out a research project. It is exciting because it gives you the opportunity to do something very personal to you. There is the freedom of not having an essay title or exam question to restrict your work, as you may have experienced in other subjects you have studied. The biggest freedom and choice you have, which also has the biggest bearing on so many aspects of your research project, is the choice of topic. Choosing a topic that you feel can successfully produce a research project is vital. Let us try a logical approach to finding a topic area.

Think about the subject matter of your academic course and possibly why you chose that course to study. Consider some of the overall aims and objectives of the course. Try and establish a big picture of the course and what you like and enjoy about it. Do you enjoy the practical coaching, testing sports people, training people or working with the community, for example? It is worth putting these thoughts on paper, or however you like. I find putting these thoughts down on paper helps make my thoughts clearer. They may remind you of thoughts of career choices too as your project can be a very strong positive to potential employers.

Now choose an interesting unit or module from your course. It should be a unit or module that you really enjoyed because it engaged your interest, and where you actively enjoyed reading about its various topics. If you have already taken the time to think and reflect about your course, identifying these modules or units will be pretty easy and should come quite naturally. If it has not, take a step back. You are building a choice based on a broad understanding, which you then need to refine to specific modules or units. Time spent doing this is worth it. Discuss your thoughts with friends, colleagues and tutors – keep bouncing your ideas around. If you have more than one unit or module that you really like, that is fine; we can apply some creativity later and there may be a potential project that covers more than one subject area, so keep them all in mind. Again it is worth scribbling these ideas down.

Sometimes it may be the way a module was taught or the character and enthusiasm of the tutor or lecturer that has made a module or unit stand out. Try not to consider this when making your choices and look deeply at the content of the module instead. The subjects and issues that were presented are what you will be working with so taking the personalities out of the equation is important so that your choices are content-based.

Reflecting on the modules or units you have identified, ask yourself which particular topics within those units you really enjoyed. You may want to look at learning outcomes for ideas of what each of the topics is specifically called (these should be clear in unit or module handbooks), or chat with tutors and lecturers about the topics they have taught.

The process of refining your decisions from the overall course, through modules or units, down to the particular topic areas within those units, should guide you towards potential research topics that engage and interest you. Jotting down the topics you liked makes it easier to discuss with particular tutors or lecturers what really interests you. Of course it may be simpler than this and you have a potential topic springing up at you from your page of writing. Importantly, however you have arrived at a topic, it should

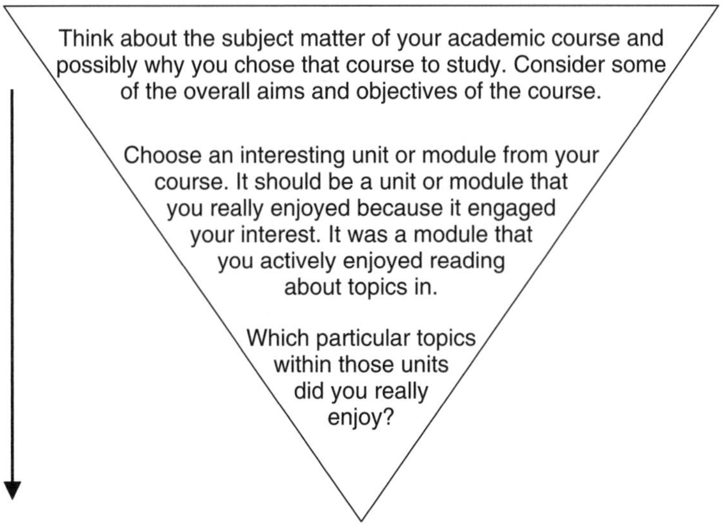

Figure 3.2 Refining your decision

be one in which you feel most confident in carrying out major independent work as well as something you wish to learn more about. Having one or two areas to consider is also all right at this point.

Learning Activity 3.1

From your work so far, create a table that lists the modules or units that you have enjoyed and engaged with. In the second column identify the topics you have particularly enjoyed in those modules or units. In a third column try to write key words that could be specific research projects. Do not be concerned if this is particularly difficult at this point; these words are the springboard for the next step in finding a research project.

If you have followed these instructions so far you are doing very well, because in three straightforward steps of logic you have identified a topic area in which you could base your research project. You may have identified more than one topic area and still have the problem of how to refine your choice down to one. I indicated earlier that this was all right and it is. If the topics you have identified are very different and there are no logical or creative connections you may have to make a simple choice. To inform that choice, you have the information you have already identified through this exercise. It is likely that choosing one topic area from a number of choices is now more a question of practicalities and motivation. If the topics have connections, why not look at potential research projects that combine the two areas? Golden rule number one for a successful project (as we saw on page 14) is to keep it simple, so try to refine the lists you have down to one or two topics maximum.

We can use some creativity as well as logical processes to help identify a potential research area and develop a question from that. The creative thing to do here is look for the links that could exist between topics. These links can provide a research area in themselves. Be creative and think more broadly than just the topics; don't be afraid to play around with the seemingly strange and utterly daft. Bounce ideas around but be careful not to manufacture something that may not have value because it seems easy. Here is one example: you may have an interest in fitness testing in one unit and also enjoyed learning about exercise in special populations. Why not consider a research project about fitness testing of special populations? Even if you finally refine an idea from this, you will still need to read to understand how this link could possibly be worked through. Remember, what you do and think must be grounded in evidence, so reading further on the two topics is important.

Golden rule number one – keep it simple

It is important for research that new and unique ideas and concepts are examined. Experienced researchers are capable of putting together series of research projects that can thoroughly examine topics. However, for you, probably doing a research project for the first time, on an academic course where the rationale for this project is for you to develop a variety of academic and practical skills, you will want to, and must, keep things simple. Do not ignore the possibility of looking again at research that has been done before and using it as a basis for your own project. At this point in your research career it is important that you choose a topic that gives you an opportunity to learn how to organise and carry out a research project, rather than aiming at lighting up the world with your originality and intellectual precociousness. So remember, keep it simple.

You may have been able to reach this point by using what you already know, with little research or reading. Before going any further take some time to read. You may want to read over particular lecture notes, or look a little more at some research articles that have been suggested as further reading for topics. Start to explore the topics with some of that intellectual curiosity that we know a good researcher needs, because now you have a little more focus on the potential topic area for your project, and you need to gain a little more background knowledge to evaluate if there is a potential research question to pursue. While reading, keep your mind open to ideas that you could potentially look at; jot down these thoughts as they occur. If after reading you find nothing has come to mind, then that was still time well spent and not wasted, because you have at least excluded a topic or two. If you find there is something interesting, again that is time well spent because you have started to find ideas. Keep your ideas to hand and don't be afraid to discuss them with others.

Refining the list of topics from many to one

If you have a few topics and some potential ideas for your research project and still cannot decide, use this list of statements/questions to help you. Honestly and frankly assess each topic that you have against the question and if you cannot agree with the statement or answer the question positively, then you should seriously consider leaving that topic for another research project on another day.

- This topic intrigues me.
- This topic interests me.
- This topic will interest the intended readers of my project.
- This topic will be able to provide enough material to meet the assigned length of the project.
- I will be able to make some useful conclusions and recommendations on this topic at the end.
- This topic can be focused and is not too broad an area.
- There is enough literature available to me to be able to carry out a literature review.
- This topic is not highly specialised.
- This topic can be researched within the resources available to me.

To answer some of these statements fully you will need to do some initial research. Remember all those resources you have available to help: your tutors, lecturers, research supervisor, peers and friends – use them to help you.

What if I can't find or think of a topic?

You may be reading this and thinking, I can't think of anything to do for my research project. Despite the previous activity you may still need help in choosing a topic; it may be that you really cannot think of anything to study. It is fine to be in this position in the early stages of the project. If it is late in the project, well, you have a lot of work to do and may be facing your first and biggest hurdle to climb over. Try these further suggestions and do not be afraid to go back to the drawing board.

Ask a tutor, friend, coach, team mate or anyone

The sooner you start to canvass opinions from those who know you well, as well as those who do not, from those who have no vested interest in your work and those who have, the sooner you will be on your way and the process will have started. Sometimes the best ideas can come from the most random people. Listen and act upon those ideas which you feel most comfortable about. Try not to be pushed into something you do not feel comfortable with. When talking to some people it is best to suggest possible ideas to start the process; it's easier to come to the table with at least some information or help them lead you through the processes we have already highlighted and see what they suggest. If you feel you have an idea that you can then go back to, considering the points highlighted above, then even better. It is really important that you do not extend this process for too long; somewhere along the line you have to bite the bullet and get down to it.

Look at previous student research work

It is very likely that your institution has examples of similar research projects that have been completed in the past. Sometimes these can be hard copies, or perhaps just a list of titles of the work done. Either way this can be enough to sow the seed of an idea from which you can grow a research project. Again, a word of warning here, particularly when looking at hard copies of others' work. It is vital that you approach this research as your own project. Remember that it is the learning that you gain from going through the process that is the important thing for you, and following somebody else's work too closely means you are being led through the dark rather than illuminating it yourself.

Develop some previous work

You may have undertaken an assignment or carried out some smaller-scale research in another of your modules or units. If you really enjoyed it, or gained some satisfaction, then consider whether it can be extended or developed fully into something that will meet the research project requirements of the institution. Your tutors may be ambivalent about this: on the one hand they will be happy that you have identified a topic on which to work, on the other they may be a little reluctant and cynical that you may just be repeating work already covered rather than developing and learning something new. Remember this when talking to them about it and consider the work you intend to do as extending the original work much further.

Look towards your own interests

Something you do outside your academic work may be the stimulus you need to develop into a research project. This could be something related to your own training or sporting interests. There have been many research projects that have come about because of a personal interest. Look at what you currently do, such as coaching or part-time work, and see if the organisations you do it for could benefit from some sort of research.

In all this keep some flexibility. It may be that you need to change direction, particularly if you start to develop an idea but meet a barrier that prevents it from progressing further. Issues such as access to young people can be an example of a barrier you may come across. There are often solutions to such barriers and your tutors and supervisors will be able to talk to you about this before you decide to change topics. Sometimes they can take some time to overcome and so try to build that into your planning. It is best to have alternative approaches to the same question or be able to take it in different directions from your initial starting point.

Even though it appears that choosing a topic to research can be a simple process, it certainly is not. Give adequate time for this process to fully occur; it may need a few weeks. You will certainly need to background read and seek opinions. Talk to your peers and hear their ideas as well as discussing your own. Everyone will want you to get this part of the whole project right first time, so take your time. In your provisional planning, why not jot down a deadline date for you to have come up with a topic?

Turning a topic into a research question

You should feel now that things can move on with your research project. You at least have a topic or possibly a few topics in your mind. Now you can think about refining and focusing these into a research question.

This is not a quick process and it will need a lot of work and input from you. It requires a lot of background reading to understand the topics and research areas more. Developing a research question may appear quite straightforward; when reading this book, it can appear that these things happen in quite an easy linear process – but think about what was said earlier. You will often need to go back and forth to refine and polish these ideas as more information and evidence helps inform those ideas. That information is absorbed through reading, so already you are gaining skills in researching topics; you should also be gaining experience in reading literature. Remember a research project is 70 per cent planning and you are only a little way in so far.

It is also likely that there will be a lot of other thoughts about your research project swimming around in your head. A good exercise here is to start to organise those thoughts, perhaps by using a mind map to help structure them. A mind map is an excellent tool that will help you organise and put some confusing thoughts to one side as you concentrate on the task at hand. From the research topic you will need to develop a workable research question, so let us start to look at what a research question is so that we understand how to turn our topic into a suitable question. A project that is based upon a research question (or a set of questions) will typically involve investigating one or more of the questions in the list below. Use this list of questions to help examine your topic in more depth. Think about whether your topic and the question can match.

- Why are things the way they are?
- What relationships exist between things?
- How should or can things be done?
- How do things work, or what is stopping them work?
- What things do, or do not exist in certain contexts?
- What is or is not going on?
- What cannot or can be done?
- To what extent is something true?

The questions are not exhaustive. Sport and exercise is a broad research area and so has many types of research questions, so you may also find yourself seeking answers to other types of questions. During this initial process of exploring research questions it is good to always consider the question, so what? Think of a potential question and imagine yourself saying it to your tutor, lecturer or supervisor. Then imagine that they simply reply with, 'so what?' It is actually a very hard question to find the answer to initially, but look for the answer in how the knowledge you will gain from asking your research question will be used. Research is all about the acquisition and creation of knowledge that has a purpose, use or application. It is answering the question 'so what?' that will help you gain confidence in what you intend to do. This is very helpful when you are faced with an inquisitive and critical supervisor.

In the same way we found a research topic there is a process we can use to turn a research topic into a question. Let us follow it using an example; try and use your own ideas in place of the example as you work through it. We will use the example of the use of caffeine. The example is there to help you work through your thoughts, not to be physiologically correct.

Conceptualise your thoughts into a directed way of thinking. This means taking your chosen topic, and understanding and describing the context or background in which the topic area and consequent problem sits and understanding some of the links in and around it.

Caffeine is a stimulant and can increase mental alertness. In many sporting activities decision making is vital to the performance outcome, the mental alertness of an individual might influence their performance, and reduced alertness would impair their performance.

State your research problem in one sentence. What is the key issue? This requires clarity of thought, an ability to focus your idea.

Increasing mental alertness, particularly late in an athletic activity, might be beneficial in sports where decision making activity is crucial.

Can this key issue be reduced to a single question? If so, what is it? This will be your research question.

Will caffeine increase mental alertness in fatigued games players?

You may have more than one question. If so, move on to the next question and use the same process. If you do have a number of questions, are they all equal in relevance or importance? Normally this would be no, and so you must identify the most important question and order the remaining ones below that. Remembering golden rule number one, keep it simple, in many cases it would be best to focus on the most important question you have identified; the other secondary questions may be useful, but for now don't let them distract you from the main focus of the project.

Review the quality with which your question encapsulates the initial thoughts as described in the first point, in terms of intellectual merit and in the context of previous research.

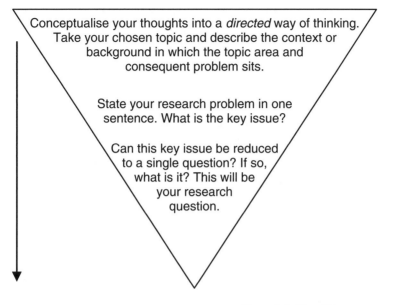

Conceptualise your thoughts into a *directed* way of thinking. Take your chosen topic and describe the context or background in which the topic area and consequent problem sits.

State your research problem in one sentence. What is the key issue?

Can this key issue be reduced to a single question? If so, what is it? This will be your research question.

Figure 3.3 Identifying your research question

Does a problem exist?

I have already stated that research is about furthering knowledge. In sport and exercise a question often raised by those who consume that research is, how can I use this knowledge? Where can it be applied? Application of knowledge is as important as the gathering of that knowledge. If you have thought about a research topic and have now developed a research question, ask yourself, where can I use the information I will find? How does it help in practical situations? It would be worthwhile to review the purposes of research in Chapter 2 to be clear as to why researching this topic or question is worthwhile. If you are in the position of not yet having a research question, your question is, do I know of a problem that needs to be examined? This can help you develop a worthwhile research question.

It would be prudent now for me to provide a word of warning. One of the biggest pitfalls in the early development of a research question is to develop a question that appears to be useful but is in fact too broad or not focused enough to be manageable and accomplished within the constraints you have. This needs to be avoided and one way to achieve this is to subject your research question to a rigorous process of interrogation. It is better for you to do this as soon as possible, because I am sure your supervisor will and it is better to have the answers ready to their questions. Remember golden rule number one – keep it simple.

Some of the questions you can ask are listed here with some advice you can consider.

- Is your question too general?

You have limited time in which to complete the research project. It is unlikely to be feasible to do justice to a general or very broad question and so you are unlikely to accomplish what you need to achieve. If your question needs three or more further questions to answer it fully then it probably is too broad. Do not abandon your ideas but try to refine and define your question further so that it becomes achievable but not too unwieldy.

A way to tighten and define your question is to look at some of the terms you use in it. An example of this is that research questions in sport and exercise may have words such as fitness or athlete in them. Both of these are very broad terms and can be made more specific. Instead of fitness, use the specific component of fitness you are examining or instead of athlete, use the specific sport you are examining. Doing this defines your research question and focuses it more tightly; the drawback can be that it also limits it. However, when you have limited resources such as time, limitation is not a bad thing.

- Is the question too tightly focused?

Having a tightly focused question will facilitate your ability to learn the research process step by step as you attempt to answer the question. If it is not focused you will find yourself being drawn away from what you set out to achieve and into different directions. However, sometimes a too tightly focused question falls into the trap of not contributing anything to the pool of knowledge as the ability to offer generalisations from the findings is too small. Remember to consider the question, so what?

What a tightly focused or a too tightly focused question is will differ from area to area of research of course. Some areas of sport, such as physiology, offer very tightly focused questions whereas sociology may naturally offer more broad questions.

- Is your question more complex than it first appears?

You may not initially see the complexity in what may appear to be a very simple question; I am sure your supervisor will, though. The complexity in the question could be that you need to establish other aspects before you can truly examine the one your question refers to or there may be possible complexities with issues such as ethics that you cannot foresee.

All potential research questions should be run by your supervisor and peers for them to offer their opinion. Remember they are valuable resources to draw upon and without expert advice it is not always easy to see what the future holds. The experience of your supervisor will help. The potential complexity of a problem does need consideration and in any research project one of the skills that will be developed is the ability to anticipate problems before they arise. That is not to say you can foresee everything but certainly a lot of problems can be anticipated and therefore dealt with before they bring the project to a halt.

Case Study

Andy had a strong interest in bio-mechanics and climbing, so his area for research and the topics he wanted to examine were easily identified. He found identifying a specific question more difficult.

I knew very quickly what I wanted to do, and discussed this with my tutor and coaches, who were all very supportive of my ideas, although I found refining my ideas and my enthusiasm into a specific manageable question more difficult. Finding relevant literature was tough and having clarity in what I really wanted to do and could manage was a long time coming.

The point Andy highlights here is that reading literature is essential to developing a specific research question but it can be difficult to find that literature. Chapter 4 will help with this.

Establishing research objectives

Now that you have worked through the tricky process of deciding on a suitable topic and developing a research question, clarity is now being added to the project. This is excellent progress and having a direction will help the enthusiasm for the project. To help with that clarity and with the planning you can also set research objectives for yourself and the project.

You should consider a research objective as something tangible, likely to actually occur in the research process, and something that you are working towards achieving. As well as research objectives, you will want to set your own objectives, such as how many participants you will recruit, and how long the data collection period will be.

Choosing a research approach: which research method should I follow?

Now you have identified a research topic, refined that to a specific question, and set objectives for your research, you have an important choice to make. That choice is which methodological route to use in order to collect data to answer the question. From research methods classes you should understand something about qualitative and quantitative research methods. It is clear that the two approaches of qualitative and quantitative research are very different in their style, language and objectives. It is likely that the ethos of your course, the modules or units you have studied, and your supervisor, will be the biggest influences upon which of the paths to follow. You will intuitively feel drawn to a method based upon your own inclinations. Some may be drawn to qualitative research because it may be seen as smaller scale, manageable and perhaps even free of statistics. It will appeal to some students because it can be perceived as being more humanistic. Quantitative research employs the same scientific principles and techniques that have made the modern world what it is and the findings from quantitative research has a definiteness that allows conclusions to be drawn. This can appeal to many researchers.

You can mix the two methods. They do not have to be exclusive. In fact such an approach offers a completeness to any project. However you do have to bear in mind the added workload in a limited timeframe when taking this type of mixed-method approach.

Writing a research proposal

All research needs to start with a definition of the research problem and that should be more easily accomplished now you have worked through the potential problems you have identified, but it is important to check and understand what exactly your institution requires of you in order to start a research project, because it is likely at some point you will be asked to produce a research proposal for your project. This is the first major milestone that you will reach and it is a very useful and significant one. A research proposal can serve many purposes, and as a researcher it is something that you should become accustomed to completing, for it is the way many research projects gain funding, through grant proposals to funding bodies for example. Writing a research proposal is a great way to start to formalise all those thoughts that you have had. It is a working document, and so some changes as it develops are to be expected, but try and think it through as far as possible and draft it a few times before you finalise the document.

As this is likely to be the first research proposal you have written it is vital that you are familiar with the requirements of your institution. Does it need to be just a half-page statement of your aims and objectives, or an outline research proposal a couple of pages long? Possibly a much lengthier piece of work is needed, perhaps including full drafts of your literature review and methodology chapters? Find out, and then use the resources of this book accordingly.

Here is a quick checklist for you to use.

- Do you have to write a full research proposal or only a statement of research aims, objectives or hypotheses?
- Is it an assessed piece of work and if so are you clear on the criteria?
- What form does it have to take, e.g. document, poster, or presentation?
- What is the word limit or required size of the proposal?
- When is the deadline for its submission?
- What happens after submission, e.g. ethics approval, etc.?

You must be clear on your institution's requirements. Once you are, look at the list below and decide what the proposal should contain. It may need some or all of these and the list is not exhaustive. The research proposal may contain:

- the context of, and rationale behind the project;
- a brief literature review;
- the methodological approach you intend to follow;
- research questions and hypotheses;
- possible methods of enquiry;
- information sources to employ;
- the significance of the project.

Writing the context of, and rationale behind the project

Whenever you write, you should consider why you are communicating this way. In writing a research proposal you are essentially attempting to convince somebody that your research project is a worthwhile one. To help to convince others that your project is worthwhile, you should provide some context or background to your study and the rationale for it, the reasons why it is worth doing.

There are three simple progressive and overlapping concepts to keep in mind when writing your background section that will help you to do this. *Engage* your readers with broader themes and topics that *illustrate* your concepts, questions, and theory and *demonstrate* your knowledge.

Engage your reader with a brief, and I emphasise brief, overview of the concepts and ideas of your topic and as you do look to make links that connect details with concepts. Use Figure 3.3, presented earlier in the chapter, to help structure this section.

You could start to sketch out your proposal ideas now. Are there written guidelines on what is required? Can you consult good examples produced by previous students? Are you sure they were working to the same criteria as you? Do you now understand what you are aiming for? If not, can your supervisor clarify it for you?

Checklist for a research proposal

- Have you developed your topic? (If not, go back and do so.)
- Have you completed sufficient background research?
- Have you understood the basic purpose of your research – is it exploratory, descriptive, or explanatory? Are your central questions descriptive, relational, or causal?
- Have you chosen to do a qualitative or quantitative study or does it combine these methods?
- Are you using primary or secondary data, or both?
- What data collection methods are you going to use?
- Do you definitely have access to the individuals, organisations or other sources (e.g. newspaper reports) that you need?
- Is your research practical? Can it be done in the time available, will it be costly, and can you do any travel that is required? Does your institution cover any costs?
- Have you worked out a timescale for your project? Is it realistic?
- Does your institution have ethical procedures that you have to comply with? Do these require clearance by senior staff? What are the timescales for this?
- Are there legal requirements that may affect your research – e.g. Data Protection Act, Children's Act?
- What types of analysis will your data require? Do you know how to do it?
- Have you proofread your proposal?
- Have you included full reference details in a consistent and approved form?

It may seem that this checklist bombards you with questions, but work through them one at a time. They are a useful reminder of how much work a project requires and what you need to do to stay on track.

Chapter Review

The take-home messages from this chapter should be:

- It is possible to develop a research area of interest by working logically through the units or modules you like, engage with, or have an affinity for, down to the content of these modules or units.

- Developing the process further, you can refine a preliminary research question. This may require some creative as well as logical thought. Any initial questions should be discussed with peers and with your research project supervisor, as they will be able to spot flaws and complexities to the question that you may not see.
- It is a good idea to set research objectives. These will help with your planning and identify whether you are on track to completion.
- Write a research proposal. Your institution may require one, but if it does not, write one anyway. A research proposal needs to convince the reader that the research project is worthwhile. To achieve this you need a clear rationale, supported by evidence, for your proposed project. Examine how to structure this and, once written, objectively test yourself by reading it and seeing if you would be convinced.

Further Reading

Berg, K (2004) *Essentials of Research Methods in Health, Physical Education, Exercise Science and Recreation.* Second edition. Baltimore: Lippincott Williams and Wilkins.

Section 2 of this text is titled Research Writing, and is very helpful when considering writing a research proposal. It is also an excellent text for those whose projects may be wider than sport and exercise science, such as health and recreation.

Thomas, J (1996) *Research Methods in Physical Activity.* Third edition. Champaign, IL: Human Kinetics.

This text is a very useful resource for research projects. Chapter 3 is very informative when considering what to include when presenting your problem.

Chapter 4
Searching for and reading research to write a literature review

Learning Objectives

This chapter will help you to be able to:

- plan, carry out and refine your literature search using concepts and synonyms;
- evaluate your literature;
- understand the requirements of a literature review.

You will also be able to:

- write a first draft of a literature review.

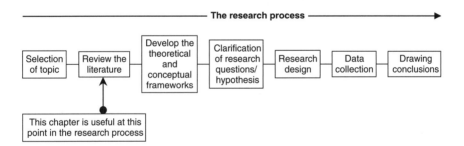

Figure 4.1 The research process: searching for and reading research to write a literature review

Introduction

This chapter is designed to help you identify, locate, read and evaluate literature in order for you to be able to write a literature review for your research project. Because any research project needs to be grounded in theory, and that understanding of theory comes from published literature, this chapter is essential reading for all.

The literature review should be considered the foundation for your research and even in the unlikely event your project does not require a literature review you must still spend time searching for and reading literature to help you settle on a research question and decide a methodological approach. Remember the definition of research, *grounded in theory*. The literature review outlines to the reader what is already known about your topic, and achieving that will also make it clearer for you. From the work done in the previous chapter, developing and refining your question, you have already started to develop the beginnings of a literature review. This chapter will take that one step further. At the end of this chapter you will be more efficient and skilled in finding, reading, and using literature in your research project.

This whole chapter is concerned with sourcing, finding and then using literature. The end point of this is to write a literature review and that should provide the reader with an explanation of the rationale for your research. It should be a balanced discussion that explains why your research is important enough to be carried out through exploration of work that has already been done. This is your way of showing that you understand where your research fits into current knowledge in the research area. This will only be possible if you are clear about what you want to research. The previous chapter will have helped you achieve that.

You have to understand where and how to search for relevant literature and how you can expand or reduce the amount of information you get. The initial part of this chapter does that. When you find relevant information it should be evaluated for its worth, and there are tips and guides on how to quickly and efficiently evaluate literature. The next part of this chapter examines the literature review.

The literature review provides the foundation for the research project, identifying the key work that is to be built upon and clarifying the theoretical and substantive focus of the research. In other words you are examining the building blocks that surround the space where your research will sit. Literature reviews are often quite difficult to write, as the amount of literature available in written and electronic form can sometimes be so overwhelming that it may be difficult to know where to start. The final section of this chapter gives guidance on how to write the literature review and discusses a method called systematic review as an alternative way to complete a literature review.

Literature

The basis of any literature review and indeed any research project is first to find the relevant literature. The literature sparks the idea, confirms your initial thoughts, or confronts your findings. Up to now you may not have used any systematic method in searching for literature but it is important that you now learn to be systematic in searching for literature. Go back to Chapter 2 and review the definition of research. I stated that it is the process of applying creative thinking in a logical way to the acquisition and creation of knowledge informed by theory and practice and informing theory and practice.

In searching for literature you will need to apply creative thinking in a logical way and as your project develops and you begin to acquire and create knowledge, you can feel confident that it is informed by theory and practice from the literature you have used. Literature reviews are about searching, sifting, sorting and evaluating literature to bring it together for the reader of your research project. Remember, *search, sift, sort and evaluate*.

Search for literature

Developing a search strategy is a logical start to finding the literature for your research project. A search strategy will also help maximise the use of one of your most precious resources, your time. A search strategy helps you to:

- define your task in terms of how much, and what type of, information you need;
- focus on your topic and exclude irrelevant information;
- modify your search, broadening out your search if you are finding too little information or narrowing your search if you are finding too much information;
- develop a systematic approach to save time when you come to revising and updating your information, or if you want to retrace your steps.

The approach and strategy I use when I undertake a search for information for a project is:

- I decide where I am going to carry out my search;
- I set a time limit for how long I will search;
- I have a list of terms written down that I will use as search terms;
- I note down the relevant details of where I have searched;
- I review my search and use it to help me learn how to search better.

I decide where I am going to carry out my search

It may be on a library catalogue or on an electronic abstract service such as Sport Discus or using an internet search engine such as Google Scholar. When deciding where to search, consider what information you are looking for. Where to search for a text book is likely to be different to where you search for a journal article.

I set a time limit for how long I will search

I try to limit searching to around 30 minutes or sometimes as much as an hour. That should be enough to gather some literature that you can actually do something with. Searching for longer produces less return for greater effort as your concentration can wane, but your initial searches as you learn and discover material may be as long as an hour.

I have a list of terms written down that I will use as search terms

This list is important and I know it will develop and change as I learn from each search I carry out, so I am prepared to look at how I should add, remove, combine different combinations of these terms to help refine or broaden my search. It is vital you remain flexible and open-minded during this process. Key terms in literature are often not the same as everyday terms.

I note down the relevant details of where I have searched

This includes details such as the location of the literature, be it a physical location or web-based resource, the date and the terms I used, and very importantly I record the details of the findings that I consider useful. This is the end product you are searching for and so care needs to be taken that you record this as accurately as possible. You may be able to access the information immediately after you have searched, or you may need to place an order for it with library or learning resource staff. In the long term you may need this information for a reference in the final report, so it is best to record as much as possible.

I review my search and use it to help me learn how to search better

You can learn from every experience you have and build your skill in searching for literature by reviewing how successful each search is. Reviewing how successful you have been and why is vital to that process of learning. If we examine each stage of the strategy I use and expand the detail, so that you follow a similar plan to mine, you too can be successful and efficient in searching for literature.

Deciding where to search for literature

In the early stages of your research project it is often best to use text books to build the foundation of knowledge before you progress further. Most institutions will have an electronic library catalogue and this should be the first place to search. If you know the actual text you are looking for, or have been recommended a text that will help and only want its location in the library, then use the title or author to do that. If you are generally looking for relevant texts then use a key word. Key words in a library catalogue can be very broad terms, such as *exercise* or *sport*. You are still likely to get quite a big return using only broad search terms but it will be a lot simpler to manage once you can identify either another broad term or a more specific search term that you can combine with it. As an example, if you are interested in older or younger athletes and sport, then search using the word *exercise*, then combine it with the word *ageing* or *youth* and the return of suitable text books is likely to be more manageable than the initial search.

If you are searching on an electronic abstract service such as Sport Discus or using an internet search engine such as Google Scholar then the search terms you use will need to be more specific to help narrow your search down from the potential millions of hits an initial search will provide. The aim when using an electronic abstract service is always to get a return of results that you are able to actually search, read and identify useful and relevant literature. If your search produces 11,452 returns, it is too broad; if it returns 17 returns then it is useful, because with 17 returns you can actually read and identify useful and relevant literature, a feat that is not possible with 11,452 returns.

It helps to always record the terms you use to search an electronic abstract service. Using words and phrases that typically would appear in the title, abstract and key word fields will help retrieve records for you to look at. You may have identified a particular author, and can search for all the work he has published. Some things to be aware of are problems you may have with plurals, such as child and children, different spellings, such as computerised and computerized, different terminology such as adrenaline and epinephrine, and words that use prefixes such as prenatal, pre natal and pre-natal.

You may prefer to use one source such as the web or the library more than another. Use Table 4.1 to compare each source.

	Library	The web
Target audience and quality of the information	Information resources have been chosen by academics to support your work, therefore you can be confident that the resources are appropriate.	Web resources are aimed at the general public and cater for a variety of levels of use. The resources are of variable quality and often unreliable.
Quantity of information	Not as vast as the web, quality over quantity.	Vast.
Organisation of information	Information is organised and there are tools, for example the catalogue that you can use to locate what you need.	Not consistently organised. No single tool comprehensively searches the web.
Cost of information	Information is free. The library has subscribed to many resources on your behalf, so the information that you find there is free to you.	Some quality resources are available on the web but often at a cost.
Help using the resources	There are many ways that you can get help including asking the library staff at the information desk and counter.	Help is more limited.

Table 4.1: The library versus the internet as a source for literature

Keep a record of your searches; it may seem more work in the beginning but as you progress it will save you so much time. Use the same template I use and look at the example in Table 4.2 to help.

Source used	**Google Scholar**
Where accessed	Via the web.
Key terms/index terms used	(Pacing, self-paced) and (exercise) and (anaerobic)
Date of your search	26th Feb 2003
Date range searched	2001 to February 2003. [It is useful to keep this detail because if at a later stage want to update yourself you may repeat the search looking for articles published outside of that time period.]
Notes	The references that resulted from searching this database have been stored in my bibliography file. Particularly interested in the article by X from ZY University so decided to see the full text and have ordered this from the National Library.

Table 4.2: A record template

I said earlier if your search produces 11,452 returns, it is too broad, and if it produces 17 returns then it is useful – but it is only useful when those 17 are all of interest. Three things that can help refine searches down to manageable amounts of records in electronic abstract services are:

- concepts and synonyms;
- Boolean operators;
- truncation symbols and wild cards.

Concepts and synonyms or key words

These may not be familiar terms to you as a potential sport and exercise specialist; they are more familiar terms to the language or computer department, but, simply put, concepts and synonyms are ideas and similar words. It is likely you use them already in your search strategies. For example, when you use a term in a search engine, that term may be very general and related to the general concept of what we are looking for. We have all done it, put in a search term to a general search engine and seen what it throws up. An example from sport and exercise physiology may be *anaerobic performance*, or from sport and exercise psychology you may have used the term *motivation*. These are both general concepts.

Learning Activity 4.1

List the general concepts for your own research. Do not try to be too specific but search for and record the broader ideas.

Often academics will prefer to use their own language and this can mean the concepts you try may actually be different to those commonly used in an academic world. The alternative words are known as synonyms. Also be aware that terminology for concepts and synonyms can be very different from country to country, particularly from the UK to the USA. One example here is that in the UK what is termed adrenaline is often referred to in the USA as epinephrine, so synonyms for adrenaline should include epinephrine.

It is important that you begin to record the key concepts and synonyms that you use and keep the results of searches where you have used them because they will help you to expand your search when you do not find a lot of information, or narrow your search when you have too much information.

Concepts and synonyms are really another way of talking about key words. Use the research papers you have already found and view the key word list; this will help you to refine and develop your own key word list.

Boolean operators

Just using the concepts, synonyms and key words you choose in different combinations will help with literature searching and the number of results you return with each combination will vary. If you look at the results you will often find hits there from unwanted sources. For example, you may be interested in a physiological aspect and that may include hits that include animal physiology, clearly not wanted for your project. There is another tool we can use that can help with our searching and this is Boolean operators.

Boolean operators are simply the terms AND, OR and NOT. Using these simple words can really increase or decrease the results we get from searches. If we use search terms from the key concepts we have developed, such as anaerobic capacity, simply typing that into many search engines finds results that contain the word *anaerobic* and *capacity* as well as the phrase *anaerobic capacity*. Try it and see how many results you get. Note the number of hits. The aim is to reduce that number to a manageable load that you can read. (It can help to use quotation marks around phrases, which tells the search engine you are looking for those words as a phrase.)

Now let us try a Boolean operator: AND. Use the phrase *anaerobic capacity* AND *sprinting*. By combining search terms and using AND, I will only find results that have the two in combination; this helps narrow my search because it includes sources with the phrase *anaerobic capacity and sprinting*, but excludes sources that may just have the word *sprinting*.

Using the OR operator is useful because it allows the use of synonyms. So I may try *anaerobic capacity* OR *anaerobic performance*. Using OR expands my search, finding sources that have synonyms.

Finally I can try NOT. This is very useful when you start to find some of the concepts and synonyms you use are used in other fields of research. Using NOT helps to remove unrelated areas. So I may try *anaerobic capacity* NOT *swimming*, so to exclude all the research that examines anaerobic capacity and swimming. This helps narrow my search.

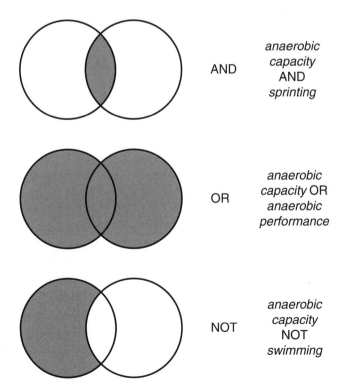

Figure 4.2 Boolean operators

Truncation symbols and wild cards

Other tools to help modify your search strategy are things known as *truncation symbols* or *wild cards*. Truncation symbols or wild cards are special symbols that have a specific role when you are searching a database. To truncate is to cut something short, and truncation symbols allow you to find words using a shorter version. The most commonly used symbols are: ?, $, +, *, # and %. Note that different databases/search facilities will use different symbols and it is always better to refer to the help pages of the particular source you are using.

Truncation symbols

A truncation symbol will allow you to search for words with the same stem, for example, *sport$*.

The $ symbol is used here to indicate that this stem is required and any letters after the stem are acceptable. A search for *sport$* would find words such as *sport, sports, sporting*. All of these words have the stem *sport*.

A truncation symbol may help you capture formats of the word that you had not thought of.

Wild cards

While truncation symbols are used at the end of words and can stand for any number of letters, wild cards can be used anywhere within a word to stand for any single letter. This is especially useful for variations in English/American spellings. With a lot of research in sport and exercise coming from America this is particularly useful and important to use when searching for literature. A search using a wild card symbol would be used in the following way: *organi*ation*. This search would return records containing the spelling variants *organisation* and *organization*. Be aware that some databases automatically make use of a wild card after a term so that plurals are found. You can usually switch this feature off.

A tip when using these tools is to look at the database help screens to find out how the wild card and truncations facilities work. Different databases/search facilities will use different symbols.

If you use something like Google Scholar's Advanced Scholar Search tool, accessible by clicking the link just next to the search window, this allows use of the same concept as Boolean operators but set out in a much simpler way.

Case Study

Do you remember Andy, the student who has recently finished a research project that examined the bio-mechanics of climbing techniques? He found identifying a specific question more difficult.

> *I knew very quickly what I wanted to do, and discussed this with my tutor and coaches, who were all very supportive of my ideas, but I found refining my ideas and my enthusiasm into a specific manageable question more difficult. Finding relevant literature was tough and having clarity in what I really wanted to do and could manage was a long time coming.*

> *I advised Andy to use some of the techniques discussed in this chapter and he did find relevant literature that helped him to develop a specific research question. We also needed to be creative and look at a broader picture as literature on his specific area was scarce.*

Evaluating and modifying your search: too much information

A common problem, particularly in the early stages, is that your searches are returning too much information. Try to notice how many returns you get for a search; often this number will be thousands, if not millions. Imagine now that there is an ideal piece of research for you at the end of that list. How likely is it that you will ever see it? Let us consider what you are doing and how can we improve it.

If you are retrieving too many resources, consider these possibilities.

- Your subject area is too broad.
- The terms you are using to define your topic are too broad. Try making them more specific, for example if you were investigating *anaerobic performance* perhaps you should add the term *sprinting*.
- Make the search more specific by adding concepts. Use the Boolean operator AND described to link concepts in your search strategy.
- Try limiting the search in some way. For example look at *sprint performance* for the previous three years only.

Evaluating and modifying your search: too little information

There will be relatively few topics that truly are difficult to find information about. It is possible the choice of topic for your research project may be a little researched area and your searches may not be returning enough hits. This is unlikely though; what is more likely is that the combination of search terms you are using is not effective. Consider the possibilities that:

- your subject area really is too narrow;
- the terms you are using to define your topic are too narrow;
- you are spelling the terms incorrectly.

The way you can correct these possibilities is by broadening the search. For example, instead of focusing on *anaerobic metabolism in sprinters* you could consider *anaerobic metabolism in runners*. To broaden it further, the search can be made more general by taking away a concept. For example, instead of focusing on *anaerobic metabolism in sprinters* you could just consider *anaerobic metabolism*. Check the terminology you used to define your concepts, particularly the spelling. Also try to identify alternative terms to express your concepts; check a thesaurus to identify synonyms and antonyms. Try using truncation so that words with the same stem but alternative endings are not being rejected. Finally ask whether you have used the most appropriate information databases for the information you need.

Sifting through the literature

The next thing is to start to sift through all the results your search has produced. A brief review of the title and abstract is normally enough to make a quick decision on whether to keep the work or not. If the abstract is promising, assess it and then look to obtain the full article, so a full reading assessment can be made. Initially you may be reluctant to reject anything but it is important that you become critical about others' work and make decisions as to what to keep and what to reject. Whilst the aim of literature reviews is to gather and use literature relevant to your research project, you can quickly be swamped so sifting through it this way initially is a good idea.

Sorting through the literature

Despite the danger of being swamped, to write a successful and effective literature review you need some material to work with. The earlier part of this chapter examined where and how to search for relevant literature. You then need to source the articles and this can and does take time. Use the resources around you to help, such as learning resource and academic staff. It can be expedient here to identify the journals that you or more senior peers may have access to and search only those journals so you can begin to write something. However, you may need to order literature and this takes time to source. If you have done this successfully you, like many in your situation, will find themselves in a position where you now have quite a big pile of research papers, journal articles, reviews, texts and perhaps other sources. If you are reading this and thinking, *I only have a few papers!*, it is likely that you have not searched effectively. The key here is to have too much rather than to have too little. Now, how do you make sense of it all, how do you sort and organise it? We need a plan.

Evaluate

Evaluate is the final part of the *search, sift, sort and evaluate* process and is about assessing literature step by step. As you begin to gather literature you must read it to assess how useful it is to your research project. There will be some that you will read and re-read time and time again, other literature you gather may be put to one side or never looked at again. How do you decide? One of the first things you should do is assess the literature. The more familiar you become with it, the quicker this process will become.

Use the headings below as a guide to logically and systematically decide whether the particular article you are reading is worth keeping. It also provides a useful self-assessment for your own report in the final draft stage.

The title and author

Does the title tell you clearly what the research is looking at? A title should be concise, direct to the point and clearly identify what the study is examining.

Do the authors seem qualified to conduct the study? Assess this by looking at the affiliations of the authors, and whether they have a reputation for research in that particular area.

The abstract

This is the author's advertisement, so to speak, for the paper as a whole, so assess it on that basis. Does it grab your attention? Do you want to read further? Does it give you an overview of the project, what the researcher did and found?

The introduction and background

Is this section helpful, comprehensive and up-to-date? Does the researcher tell you why this subject interested them? Has the researcher justified why the research was worth doing?

The literature review

Does the literature review give you an insight into the current state of knowledge about this subject? Is it fair and unbiased? Is it structured in such a way as to be accessible? You will need to check on at least a sample of the references. This section is often restricted in length by the journal.

The method

Is it described clearly? Does it seem to be the correct approach and method? Are any ethical issues clearly addressed? Could this study be repeated from the description given in the report? How was the sample selected? Is the sample representative or, even more simply, big enough?

The analysis and results

What method was used to analyse the results? Do the numbers add up? Does the presentation of the results illuminate or baffle? Has the researcher used the right analysis tool?

Don't be frightened by the use of statistics and don't assume the researcher knows any more than you about statistics. A vital thing to remember here is if the material going into the statistics is not very good, then the material coming out of the statistics will be poor too. Remember, *garbage in, garbage out*.

Discussion

Does the discussion derive from the results or just wishful thinking on the part of the author? Are the conclusions clearly stated? How does the discussion relate to the literature? Is the discussion sensible or is the researcher on another planet?

Recommendations and conclusion

This section is often combined with the discussion but comes towards the end of it. Are the recommendations directly related to the results? For example, are they in tune with the scale of the study or too global? Has the researcher critiqued the study? What next? Has the researcher suggested future study or can you think of any?

Acknowledgements

You may find clues here about the real purpose of the study or expert assistance.

References

Are they comprehensive, relevant, up to date and correctly cited? How many times has the author cited their own work?

Overall communication

Considering who the report is aimed at, is the style appropriate to the audience? Is it accessible? Is it well written? Is it published in the right forum? In research there is often very technical language, the assumption is other researchers in that field will understand that language; however, there is a difference between jargon and the legitimate terminology of research. You should be sceptical of the first but must learn the second in order to communicate well.

Two other areas that are worth considering when evaluating a research article are:

- *Bias.* Why has the researcher done the study? Is there an underlying agenda that might bias the whole study?
- *Ethics.* Does the study satisfy ethical requirements?

> ### Learning Activity 4.2
>
> Look for two papers that you are considering using in your research; choose one by an author well known to you, and choose another by a more obscure author. It would be helpful if they were published reasonably close together in time. Use the criteria above to assess both papers. The results from that assessment may now make you think more critically about the quality or worth of a particular paper. This exercise is worth repeating later on, particularly if you have to reduce the amount of research you intend to include in your report.

The literature review

The literature review should provide the reader, and perhaps more importantly at this point your tutor or supervisor, with an explanation of the rationale for your research. It should be an argument that explains why your research is important enough to be carried out as well as a critique of the work of others in a similar field. This is your way of showing that you understand where your research fits into current knowledge in the area you are researching. This will only be possible if you are clear about what you want to research. So if you are not 100 per cent confident and do not have a very clear outline of what you are doing, you should not start writing the literature review. That is not to say that you should not be collecting, reading and digesting literature that will help you – you should be doing that.

Literature reviews can be and are often quite difficult to write, as the amount of literature available in written and electronic form can sometimes be so overwhelming that it may be difficult to know where to start. Indeed, one of the important skills that you will develop as a researcher is the ability to identify what literature is appropriate to your research and what is not. This is a skill that needs to be developed and it will be as you continue on this journey.

It is very important that you know what you need to do. What is it your institution requires you to do? Use these questions to prompt you to be clear in your mind as to what your own institution asks of you when writing a literature review.

- What form must the literature review take?
- Is there a word limit?

- Is there a deadline?
- Will your supervisor read a draft?
- What resources are available from your institution's library?
- Do you have a subject librarian or a learning resource assistant who can help?
- Do you know which referencing method is required of you?

Recording and evaluating your literature review sources

Earlier in the chapter I dropped the hint that it would be worth beginning to record all the details of the papers and journal articles that you are gathering together. There was even an example form to use. Many of the electronic databases you have searched allow you to keep an electronic record of the searches and results. You can often e-mail this to yourself. This is very useful of course. To help with writing your literature review, you can add to your record thoughts or ideas about how that particular piece of literature can contribute to the literature review.

However you choose to record your literature is down to you, your skills and your institution's resources. Let me explain. Remember Chapter 2 stated that one of the essential personal qualities of a researcher is to be organised. If you have already started to keep a record of the research papers because you are that type of person then that's great, if you are not, this is a personal quality you need to develop. It may be that you have good IT skills, if so then developing a system of recording all the information you need about your growing collection of research papers may be something that comes easily to you. Many people use an IT database to help them collate and record their research papers. Equally, if your IT skills are not too well developed, you can use a spreadsheet or even just keep a document with all the references written down. It is best if they are in the referencing format required by your institution; that way you can cut them and paste them into your report when needed. Your institution may have a commercial software referencing package loaded onto its computers. If it has then you really should spend some time learning how to use it. The time you will save and the benefits you will gain far outweigh any difficulty you may have in the beginning. However you choose to record your references, it is essential that you do. Why? Because when you come to compile your reference list in the write-up of your research report or dissertation you can bet the one reference you really need will be the one you cannot find.

Reflection Point

Sarah completed a research project in sport and exercise and I remember clearly her comments when I discussed with her how she found the process.

I wish I had been more organised. I think my data collection was well organised, because I had to be for the sake of other people. When it came to my writing up I really needed to be organised with all the papers I had collected. The time I spent looking for this reference or that reference sent me mad. It wasn't a nice feeling with deadlines looming.

The point Sarah highlights here is clear. With some organisation early on a lot of time could be saved later when you really need it. This is the type of advice that only someone who has been through the experience can give.

What to record?

I would suggest as a start, record the minimum amount of detail that you will require for your institution's referencing requirements unless you use a referencing software package. Use a template to keep it the same for every source and remember that each source may require supplemental information, particularly if it is an electronic source. Normally you will be able to find examples of particular reference styles for different sources. Your institution may even have their own guide, or consult with the learning resource staff.

Template for recording references

Author(s)   _____

Year of publication   _____

Title of article   _____

Journal title   _____

Volume and issue   _____

Page numbers   _____

This would be the minimum amount of information to record. I find it useful to also record some notes and thoughts about particular research papers or articles. I also use a mind map to help me organise my literature in the different sections of the literature review that I consider relevant.

Read the following section on systematic review and you may feel you would like to add some more information into your record of literature. Before you add anything think about the inclusion and exclusion criteria you will be using because these are the key factors that decide if literature stays or goes. For example you may decide that factors such as the number of participants studied, the experimental design used, or the experimental method, are important.

Systematic review

Systematic review of the literature is a very useful method of ensuring the literature you review is the most vital and valuable literature for your study. A systematic review is an overview of primary studies that used explicit and reproducible methods. That means it overviews the studies that produced primary data in a very clear and reproducible way. You set the criteria for the inclusion and exclusion of literature.

Not all research topics suit the use of a systematic review so before you embark on a systematic review it is important you consider whether the topic area and subsequent literature you have to date lends itself to this method.

A systematic review tries to bring as high a level of rigour to reviewing research evidence as should have been used when producing that research evidence in the first place. In a systematic review you will take great care to find all relevant studies, assess and synthesise the findings from individual studies in an unbiased way and present a balanced and impartial summary of the findings with due consideration of any flaws in the evidence. By following this approach you may suddenly find some of the research that you may not have questioned previously has not all been produced with meticulous care, and therefore the findings may be questionable. By interrogating published reports and asking a series of questions you can uncover deficiencies.

If you are using the systematic review method then you will have a set of inclusion and exclusion criteria. Using this type of criteria helps avoid potential bias when reviewing literature and can help in ensuring objectivity. You now, if you have not already, start to read and digest what the literature's key points and findings are. Make notes as you do this; it will really help when you write up and it helps prompt the thought process. You should also be able to organise literature into a more structured way. Placing articles into groups, perhaps by approach or another area, is useful. You may be lucky enough to have articles with rebuttals and this can be very useful when assessing literature.

Review papers

Sometimes in very popular areas of research a researcher may gather together a large amount of studies and attempt to review them in one go. These are called review papers and can be very useful, especially if this is your first research project and you need to gather an understanding of a large topic in a well-structured way. In sport and exercise you will see review papers, and many of them will be narrative reviews. There are some drawbacks to narrative reviews such as:

- they are by nature subjective and therefore prone to bias and error;
- without guidance by formal rules, different reviewers of the same topic can disagree;
- issues as basic as what types of studies to include or not in a review;
- how to balance the quantitative evidence they provide;
- selective inclusion of studies that support the author's view.

So using a systematic approach to reviewing literature may help overcome some of these drawbacks to narrative reviews.

It is also useful to assess literature for its standard and quality with sometimes less objective criteria. A common mistake is to believe that simply because it is published the researchers must have done something worthwhile; this is not always the case and as researchers we need to be aware that we do not fall into the trap of believing everything that glitters is gold. Start to assess the literature critically, and give weight to the literature you find worthwhile in your own mind. Use questions such as the following:

- What is the source? Is it an international peer-reviewed journal or an unknown website? Which would have more weight in your thinking?
- Who are the authors? Have they published work in a similar area?
- Have others used this literature in their own work? How many people have cited it?
- When was the article published? Is it recent?
- Overall, how *good* do you think the article is?

Have confidence that the more you read and understand relevant literature in your chosen area, the more you will begin to develop expertise in that area. Use that confidence to express an opinion as to the usefulness and relevance of the literature you read, but remember you need to support your criticisms.

How to write the review

Now, like any essay you have previously written, the key to writing something successfully is to plan it prior to starting and be prepared to draft and revise as it develops. You could start to use the mind map that you previously developed to help organise how the literature review should be structured.

Overall your literature review should begin with broad topics that are connected with the subject but are not covered in any depth in the review. This gives the reader an introduction to the topic before you start to look at material in more depth and complexity. It is also worthwhile in many cases to set the literature review in context. You may have already done this in the introduction section but it is worthwhile repeating it to help set the scene. In the same way that you are starting with what the literature review will cover, do not be afraid to state what it will not cover. There may be aspects which you have not examined as they have no relevance to your study but do have relevance to the topic area. An example of this is that you may, for instance, be covering the use of caffeine as a supplement. Your literature review will concentrate on its use as a supplement to improve performance but will not examine the health aspects of using it. Here refer the reader to relevant literature, if you know of it, so they can read it if they wish.

The next part of your literature review should then start to examine the literature specific to the research question. Here you can begin to discuss the relevant findings of other research, demonstrating how they do or do not contribute to your ideas and development. Remember the literature review provides the foundation for your research project or dissertation. Its purpose is really to identify the key works upon which you are basing your research project or dissertation. It clarifies the theoretical concepts you are using to justify your own ideas. The literature review outlines what is already known about your topic and where your research fits within this. So the final part of writing the literature review highlights the critical information that leads to your research question of the hypothesis of the study.

There are key ideas when constructing a literature review. Consider it to be a funnel where you lead the reader from the broad themes, to information more specific to the topic, and finally present the critical information that leads to your research question or the hypothesis of the research project if applicable. You can also construct each particular section in the same way. Using this funnel helps you take the reader to an inevitable conclusion with supporting evidence:

- broad topics;
- specific topics related to your area;
- critical information.

Use these questions to prompt you to consider how you have written your literature review. Why not give your literature review to your peers and ask them to rate you using these questions as a prompt?

- Have you used an appropriate mix of sources, for example, books, journals and web sources?
- Have you used recently published information?
- Have you used credible sources of information, for example, academic journals or research texts?
- Have you covered the main concepts that are pertinent to your research?
- Have you considered all relevant arguments?
- Is the material you have used always relevant for your project?

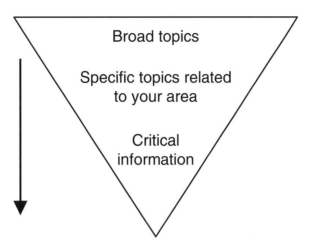

Figure 4.3 Reaching a conclusion through funnelling

- Have you made a clear argument for your research?
- Do you have concise research questions as a result of the review?
- Have you used references to support your arguments?
- Is the literature review all your own work?

Things not to do in a literature review

Do not simply describe

It is difficult at times to remember how you have grown in confidence and ability throughout your studies and it is likely that if you are writing up a research project or undertaking a dissertation you are at the pinnacle of your studies to date. So if you are it is unlikely that simply describing other studies or even just comparing and contrasting them is enough at this level.

Reading literature and absorbing the learning you have gained should give you the confidence in your chosen area that you can now express opinions, supported by evidence, that some studies may be more valid than others, or that some of the methods used by some research is more applicable and reliable than others. I would suggest that after the first draft you review what you have written with the critical question in your mind, *Have I synthesised and reflected upon the research of others?* Feel confident to express your opinion, always supported by evidence.

Do not structure chronologically

Structuring a literature review chronologically can appear a sensible and logical way to do it. However, only in a few cases is it an appropriate method. Structuring a literature review chronologically can often make it appear very stilted to the reader and the synthesis of information needed can often be difficult if chronological structuring does not run in the right order for the particular point you wish to use.

Mistakes to avoid in a literature review

- Do not make the review simply a list of past studies. Ensure that the literature you review is related to your study and not simply a general review of the subject matter.
- Make sure that you have taken time to identify the best sources of literature and given each source that you use the due weight it deserves.
- Make sure that you have understood and demonstrated how your literature relates to the relevant wider picture. Make sure you have answered the *so what?* question.
- Do not uncritically accept the findings of existing literature. Make sure you critically evaluate them.
- Make sure you have considered contrary findings and alternative interpretations.
- If you have raised problematic issues, have you addressed them?

Ensure you:

- know what form the literature review must take;
- have made a convincing argument for your research;
- have structured your argument well;
- have proofread your literature review;
- have included full reference details in a consistent and approved form;
- have laid the review out clearly.

Chapter Review

The take-home messages from this chapter should be:

- You should have a logical method to search, sift, sort and evaluate the literature you use. A little time spent recording your searches and recording your thoughts on how the literature will fit into your literature review in these early stages will save incredible amounts of time later in the project.
- When searching for literature you should be creative in the terms you use. If you are finding too much or too little literature, use tools such as Boolean operators to help limit or expand your search. Remember if you are using electronic sources, the fewer relevant hits you return, the more able you are to evaluate that literature.
- Begin to develop a method to critique the work of others. Simply because it is published does not make something a high quality resource. You may spot flaws, ways it could be improved, or omissions, which your research project may address.
- When writing your initial draft of your literature review, consider how you will structure it, and how the literature you have will fit into that structure. Then consider the structure of the sections within that draft. Always consider the reader of your work. Every time you write you are taking that reader down a path to a conclusion. Look for how you can show them the path, lead them down it, and guide them to the same end you have reached.

Further Reading

There are many excellent texts that will contribute to your understanding of how to search for and evaluate literature, as well as how to structure and write a literature review. Below are texts specific to sport and exercise which I would recommend.

- Gratton, C and Jones, I (2003) *Research Methods for Sport Studies.* London: Routledge.
- Long, J (2007) *Researching Leisure, Sport and Tourism. The essential guide.* London: Sage.

There are also many excellent texts that are not specific to sport and exercise but can help greatly with searching, evaluating, and using literature. Two I would recommend are:

- Pritchard, A (2008) *Studying and Learning at University. Vital skills for success in your degree.* London: Sage.
- Barrass, R (2002) *Scientists Must Write.* Second edition. London: Routledge.

Chapter 5
Designing an experiment

This chapter will help you to be able to:

- select the appropriate experimental design for your research project;
- understand what a cause and effect relationship is;
- understand the concepts of reliability and validity in an experimental context.

You will also be able to:

- identify the different types of experimental design that could be used.

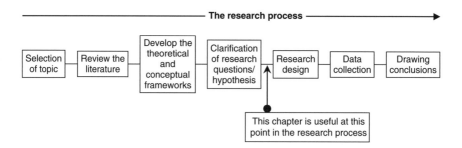

Figure 5.1 The research process: designing an experiment

Introduction

If your research project is going to use an experiment to gather the data for your results, then this chapter is for you. Chapter 3 will have helped you clarify your particular research question and from this you can determine the most appropriate research approach. Non-experimental research is covered in the next chapter. If you have determined that you are following an experimental research approach, then you need to read and understand this chapter. This chapter will aid you in designing an experiment that will answer your question in the most appropriate way. Experimental research normally tests a hypothesis. If you are not sure if your research should have a hypothesis or not, then it is important that you go back to Chapter 3 to develop your research problem further.

It is a basic premise that experiments are designed to establish causality. Causality is where one thing has an effect on the other, simply, that X causes Y. This chapter begins by examining what a cause and effect relationship is and then discusses how to design an experiment that will establish one, if one exists. Experiments can also be used to examine relationships, where the mechanism or causality of that relationship can be determined.

To establish causality we need to understand what the experimental method is. We may find out that not all experiments take place in a laboratory, especially in sport and exercise. This chapter also examines the premise behind the experimental method.

To make any eventual conclusions worthwhile it is important that the raw data we have collected is accurate and free, as much as possible, from any error. We will look at what measurement error is and, using some examples, we will help you understand what you can do to minimise it in your own research project. By looking at measurement error we will also be able to put the concepts of reliability and validity into the context of your own research project.

Finally, we will examine the different types of experimental design. We do this because it is from these general designs that you will choose your experimental design, or you may design one yourself that is best suited to your research project based on one of these designs. Consider the experimental design as the blue-print from which you will construct your research project. If you start with a good blueprint you are more likely to build a good research project.

Causality, experimentation and establishing a cause and effect relationship

We know from Chapters 3 and 4 that it is previous research and the published literature, in and around our subject area, that informs our opinions on what may or may not cause something to happen. Reading and understanding this literature causes questions to be raised in our minds, such as, *What if this was added?*, or *What would happen if it was tried this way?* and so on. This thinking was the beginning of our research question which we have since developed. When we develop these questions further to propose a hypothesis we are, sometimes more intuitively, suggesting that something may cause an effect on something else. When we do this we have already identified some key principles of research. That is, we have identified our independent and dependent variables.

An independent variable is something that is manipulated by the researcher to see the effect upon a dependent variable. A dependent variable is something we measure. So what we are actually saying is we manipulate a potential cause to measure an effect. Let me make this really clear. If I have designed an experiment where I want to measure the effect of a sports drink on endurance performance, the independent variable is the sports drink. It is independent because it is just what it is, a sports drink. It is independent of where it is used. It could equally be a new performance-enhancing supplement or a new training method. The researcher manipulates the sports drink by deciding who to give it to in a single event. Now, when that sports drink is given to a performer, then you could expect to see an effect on their performance; this effect is the dependent variable. They may run further or faster in that event. The dependent variable is the measure; we would measure the distance or time. It is important that you understand independent and dependent variables as they play a big role in experimental research.

Experimentation allows for the development of new knowledge by introducing and then manipulating an independent variable to produce an effect on a dependent variable. Where we are confident that any effect on a dependent variable is caused by the independent variable, we have a cause and effect relationship. A sports drink causes endurance performance to improve, for example. It seems simple that we can establish causality and demonstrate that a cause and effect relationship exists, but that can only be true when we are sure that it really exists because we have controlled or eliminated all the other possible causes and influences. Some of these other possible causes or influences are known as extraneous variables.

In a simple example you may want to examine the effect of training programmes, the independent variable, on fitness levels, the dependent variable. This simple idea becomes more complex when we start to consider how often they should train, at what intensity, etc. These considerations and the decisions you make can be informed by reading the research of others. Consider also how their work or other activity may influence the results. This is the effect of extraneous variables. You need to develop a keen eye for the levels of control within your work.

In this example when we review our research it is important that we are confident that the training we have designed really is the reason there was an improvement in fitness levels. There is always a possibility that results seen are by chance or that another influence, an extraneous variable, has affected the outcome. Experimentation should be performed with a careful and systematic approach to minimise as much as possible those threats to validity. Minimising threats to validity increases confidence that any effect seen is because of the manipulation of the independent variable. Only when it can be logically determined that one factor produces a predictable influence on another is a cause and effect relationship said to exist.

If a cause and effect relationship is seen, robust repeated experimentation by others will confirm that this relationship is correct. This is also why it is acceptable to often repeat the studies of others; science is about reproducibility. However, it is not only about determining the present, what is seen here and now, but also about being able to generalise the relationship to conditions and situations outside the experiment with confidence, thereby allowing prediction of future events.

The experimental method

You may be keen to jump right in and start to design an experiment that appears to do what you want. Taking this approach gets on with the job but you find that many mistakes will be made that cannot be rectified later, so hold on, be patient. So, before we can design and carry out our experiment, we need to understand what we mean by the experimental method.

The experimental method of research is where a variable is manipulated and the effect of that manipulation is observed. Consider something like a strength training programme to help understand this. We would manipulate the weight lifted, by increasing it or by increasing the number of repetitions or sets over time and observe the increase in strength. The manipulation of the weight training programme by weight, repetitions, sets or any combination of these is the independent variable and the growth in strength, or not, is the observed effect of that manipulation, the dependent variable.

When we decide to observe the effects of manipulation of variables we have the choice to observe that either under known, tightly defined and controlled conditions, like in a laboratory, or as they would be under natural occurrence, like that which occurs in actual sport performance. This choice that we have is the start of the *basic* versus *applied* debate in sports research. Do we observe a performer in very unnatural conditions, like in a laboratory on a treadmill or other equipment, or should we observe them in the natural field of performance? This is another of the many choices that you have to make in your research project. There is no right or wrong as to where in the spectrum you choose, just different advantages and disadvantages.

Experimental research and sport

Let's look at some typical examples of experiments in sport. We will use these examples throughout the chapter. Try to always put your own research project in the context of these examples and perhaps make some notes to aid you as you do.

Example 1

If we give a group of people a training programme to follow over a period of weeks and observe the fitness levels of the group, both prior to and at the end of the programme, we may expect to see a difference in fitness levels at the end of the programme. By allowing people to follow a training programme without too many controls and restrictions on their daily lives the result is more representative of what normally happens. This is observing changes as they would be under more natural conditions. This is research that is further towards the *applied* end of the spectrum.

The training programme is the variable we can manipulate and the change in fitness levels the observed effect. One way to do this as an experiment is to take a group and measure fitness levels before they start, allow them to do the training programme, and then measure fitness levels at the end. The problem here is if they are allowed to be in *natural* conditions, how sure can we be that any changes in fitness levels are due to the training programme and not another influence, an extraneous variable?

We could take the group as a whole and divide it into two. Then, by asking some participants to follow the programme and others not to and observe the changes of fitness levels of both groups, we can compare differences between groups and be more confident that changes that occur are due to the training programme. This is an example of how we can design our experimental method. We may decide to manipulate the training programme in other ways with more groups, the amount of training they do, at what times and for how long, but if we start to do this we make things more complicated.

The training programme experiment is an example of an experiment where we expect to see a difference. That is the participants who follow the training programme should show higher fitness levels at the end than the group who did not.

Example 2

We can take a participant, or even better a group of participants, in the laboratory and carefully increase running speed on a treadmill and measure blood lactate levels at set regular points until the participant reaches exhaustion. This manipulating of the variable of treadmill speed under known, tightly defined and controlled conditions then observing the changes in blood lactate levels is an example of more *basic* research.

The treadmill speed is the variable we manipulate as we increase its speed and the blood lactate level is what we observe. How we decide to manipulate the treadmill speed, by how much it increases, and how often and for how long we ask the participant to run at that speed is an example of how we design our experimental method. We could build on this design by measuring other participants and observing their responses to increases in treadmill speed and collecting all that data together as a whole group.

In this experiment we may expect to see a relationship between what we manipulate and what we observe in the participants. As we increase running speed on a treadmill and measure blood lactate levels at regular points until exhaustion we expect to see a relationship between running speed and blood lactate levels.

Consider both examples. One looked for a difference; the other looked for a relationship. The question, *Am I looking for a difference or a relationship?* is important to answer as soon as possible, and it is important that we understand some of the complexities contained in it. If we have two separate groups, such as a training and a non-training group, we may look for a difference between those groups. In this example we may be able to clearly identify a cause and effect type of relationship. If we have two separate variables, such as lactate and running speed, we may look for a relationship. We cannot be sure that the relationship we see is caused by one or the other variable; in some cases it will be, in others it will not.

It seems straightforward so far. Now we consider using one group which we may test in two conditions. An example of this would be a sports drink experiment. We take a group of athletes, test them on time taken to complete 10,000 metres running *without* the sports drink, then a week later test them again on time taken to complete 10,000 metres running *with* the sports drink. We may expect to see a difference in the times, but also because the same athlete does both tests we may expect to see a relationship between improvements in time and amount of drink consumed. These are just examples of considerations that we have to think through before we can go forward with the design of our experiment.

The experimental method and protocols

How we actually put our participants through the experiment is called the protocol. To design a protocol and follow an experimental method we need to understand the variables, the things that can change or stay constant, to ensure our protocol and experiment gathers data on what we are examining.

Already in the examples we have seen we have identified variables, such as training programmes and running speeds, and effects we may observe, such as changes in fitness levels and blood lactate. Using our knowledge of the subject area we can intuitively make a prediction of what we may expect to observe following manipulation of a variable. We may expect to see a difference in fitness levels between those who do the training programme and those who do not, or we may expect to see a relationship between blood lactate levels as running speed increases. These intuitive predictions are the beginning of the development of hypotheses.

What we need to ensure before we continue is that we can clearly identify in our hypothesis the variables we manipulate and the effects we are going to observe. In a hypothesis, the variable we manipulate is the *independent variable* and the effect we observe is the *dependent variable*. Hypotheses will have one or more independent variables that you will manipulate and you will have an objective measurement, a dependent variable that is the effect of this manipulation. All this talk of variables and hypotheses can seem confusing, but let us consider two examples.

A hypothesised difference

We can hypothesise that there will be significant difference in fitness levels between groups who do a training programme compared to those who do not train. The independent variable, the one we can manipulate, is whether a group trains or not. The dependent variable, the objective measurement you can make, is the degree of fitness of the group. It is important to notice here that we are looking for a *difference between* two groups.

A hypothesised relationship

We can hypothesise that there is a significant relationship between running speed and blood lactate levels. The independent variable is the speed of the treadmill. The dependent variable is their level of blood lactate.

	Hypothesis	Independent variable	Dependent variable
Experiment that looks for a difference between measurements	There will be significant difference in fitness levels between a group that do a training programme compared to a group who do not train.	Whether a group trains or not – in this case this variable has two levels.	Degree of fitness.
Experiment that looks for a relationship in measurements	There will be a significant relationship between running speed and blood lactate levels.	Running speed.	Blood lactate levels.

Table 5.1: The relationship between independent and dependent variables

Learning Activity 5.1

This activity is designed to help you identify your independent and dependent variables. The first part of this task is to state definitively what your experiment is aiming to find, a difference or a relationship. Then create a table of three rows and two columns, and in the first column list the following:

- my hypothesis is . . . ;
- my independent variable is . . . ;
- my dependent variable is . . . .

In the column next to these headings identify the statements you need to make. It would be worthwhile checking these with friends or perhaps your tutor or supervisor to ensure you are correct.

Now you have clearly identified your independent and dependent variables you could start to think about what methods you could use to measure them. Create a list of action points from this work.

Error and how to control it

Let's explore a little more about what we can do to ensure an experiment is likely to produce data that we can use before we begin to look at how to design one.

> The more complex the science, the more essential is it, in fact, to establish a good experimental standard, so as to secure comparable facts, free from sources of error.
>
> (Bernard, 1949)

From this quote we can deduce that even the simplest science, the simplest experiment, to produce worthwhile results needs a good experimental standard – but what exactly do we mean by *good experimental standard*? A good experimental standard is one where we should aim to carry out an experiment free from sources of error.

An experiment has something which we manipulate (our independent variable) and something we observe that shows the effect of that manipulation (our dependent variable). What we should aim for is that the measurement of our dependent variable should be a *true* score, which is one that is free from error.

If we take a dependent variable and look at what could influence it in an experiment, what we see is that we actually have a measurement that has:

- a *true* score;
- *systematic error*, that is, some error added to the true score that is systematic, in that it affects all the scores in a similar way. An example of systematic error can be using weighing scales that are a few kilograms out. As long they are not adjusted they will always remain the same number of kilograms wrong. The error is systematic and is always produced, as long as things do not change.
- *random error*, that is, some error that adds to the true score that occurs randomly. Random error can result from the experimenter reading a score incorrectly, for example.

An experiment would want measurements as close to the *true* score as possible. If there is too much error, whether systematic or random, then our measurements are not likely to be valid. If it has a lot of random error then it will not be reliable. See the section on *threats to internal validity from equipment* later in this chapter for some examples of random and systematic error.

The question you have now is, *how do I ensure I measure my dependent variable as close to the true score as possible?* For this text to be specific to your study is very difficult as every research project will differ and require a slightly different approach. It is something that should be discussed with your tutor or supervisor. Generally, I can recommend that you maximise your measurements' validity. This will certainly help in avoiding error.

Maximising your measurements' validity

This section will help you understand the concepts of reliability and validity better because you will place them into the working context of your own experiment.

As a researcher any experiment we carry out has to have internal validity and external validity. Internal validity is the degree to which we can be sure that the measurements we have and can show are due to manipulation of the variables and not something else. External validity is the degree to which we can generalise what we find in our experiment to the general population.

Let us use the earlier examples of training programmes affecting fitness levels and running speed affecting blood lactate levels to help us understand the threats that can occur to internal and external validity.

Threats to internal validity from your sample group

Your sample is the selected participants drawn from the population under investigation. If the sample undertaking the fitness programme is very different to the sample chosen to do no training then there is a danger we may be measuring differences that are there to start with, not any differences that come about because of the training programme. This can be controlled by randomly assigning people into groups; random assigning evens out differences. Sometimes you may have a study that requires groups to be different. You may be looking at age differences or differences between genders. In this type of research project, threats to internal validity from the sample group are unavoidable but should be discussed to show you understand the principle.

Another threat to consider under this heading is the consideration of participant drop out. This is also rather scarily known as differential mortality. It is inevitable that you are likely to lose some participants from your sample. It may be that some of the participants you lose were all those upon whom your treatment, manipulation of the independent variable, had an effect. This will affect the results and make them invalid. To help with this you should aim to over-recruit participants for your study.

Reflection Point

Paula, a student who has recently finished a research project that examined the effect of music on training performance, commented:

I realised very early that a lot of the people I expected would be participants for me were also going to be busy with their own research projects. I was lucky in that I had a squad of netball players I could call upon to be my participants. A lot of my friends struggled to get enough participants though.

The point Paula makes is that you need to think about participant recruitment early in your study.

Threats to internal validity from time

Things naturally change over time, and so how your experiment is designed and the timing of when you take measurements is crucial. If we use the example of blood lactate, the time course of how blood lactate levels are reflected in blood taken at a sample site is important to understand so that when measurements are taken they are likely to be an accurate reflection of what is actually happening. Equally, with training programmes fitness levels change over time. Expecting to see changes after only one week is unlikely, but measuring fitness levels six weeks after they have finished is also likely to produce invalid results.

Threats to internal validity from history

When we talk of threats to internal validity that arise from history, we are referring to events that could occur in the lives of the participants that are unrelated to our manipulations of the independent variable, which could give rise to changes similar to those we are expecting. An example of this would be if one of the training participants' car was to break down and they had to walk to work for six weeks – they might get fitter as a result of this. We would not be able to fully determine the extent to which they got fitter because of our training programme or because of the fact they were walking more. This may be unavoidable but asking participants relevant questions can help indicate if it occurs. So in physiological studies you may ask participants when the last time they exercised was, or other questions relevant to the factors you are examining.

Threats to internal validity from equipment

The results that you measure can only be as good as the equipment you use to measure it and how familiar you are with that equipment. Doing a research project, perhaps for the first time, means it is likely that you will be using some equipment for the first time. As you become more familiar with the equipment, the more often you use it, you may begin to be less careful about its operation and so random error may start to creep in. This can result in data which become more and more invalid over time. Another possibility is that you fail to calibrate the equipment prior to using it or ensure it remains calibrated, so that any measurements you take are invalid. This can result in systematic error.

Threats to internal validity from reactivity and experimenter effects

Because sport research deals mainly with human participants, whenever you place a person in an experimental situation it is likely this will affect their behaviour. A common example of this is how a person's blood pressure often shows a higher reading caused by the stress of having their blood pressure measured. This type of reactivity to an experimenter threatens the validity of the results and so should be reduced. You may wish to carry out some familiarisation trials with the participants prior to actually carrying out the data collection. These familiarisation trials are where the participant is brought in, shown what is going to happen and in some cases allowed to have a go, a trial run if you like. It reduces their anxiety and is also good practice for you.

It is also likely as a young researcher that you will use people you know as participants in your study. Why not? These are people who are friends and often willing participants but potentially you could influence those people as an experimenter because the participant may try to please you by attempting to make the experiment work. One method to reduce this effect is the use of a double blind design. This is where the experimenter and the participant are both unaware of which condition the participant is in. Unfortunately it is unlikely that the resources for this to happen in student research will be available, therefore you should employ at least a single blind design. This is where the participant is unaware of which condition they are in.

Other threats to internal validity

There are other threats to internal validity from other considerations but these are less likely to occur in research into sport and exercise. Considerations such as maturation, the changes that will occur as people naturally develop, are particularly important in studies of children over time. Another possible threat is regression to the mean. This is where participants or observations produce extreme, either high or low, measurements on a pre-test or occasion by chance. Consequently they are likely to produce scores closer to the mean on a subsequent test and this regression, moving back, to the mean, can be misinterpreted as an effect when it is not.

Take some time to now consider your project. What are the potential threats to validity to your research? Draw a mind map to help you consider them. They can be very useful because all the questions asked make you think of what needs to be considered and found out.

Threats to external validity

It is best to highlight here two threats to external validity that are likely to occur in research projects. Remember external validity is the degree to which we can generalise what we find to the general population:

- the overuse of special participant groups;
- restricted numbers of participants.

In research projects you will tend to look for participants from your own peer group or local area. This is likely to mean that participants are reasonably fit, young, and possibly more intelligent than the normal population. Using these participants for research limits the ability to be able to generalise to the population because the population as a whole are not as fit, young, and possibly intelligent as you. The other common occurrence in student research is the limited number of participants a study will use. This will affect the reliability but also affects the ability to generalise to the population. Sample size is an important factor in finding statistical significance. Now that you have a clearer idea of threats to validity and reliability, what are you going to do next?

Experimental research

If we want an experiment that is free from error, one thing will help, that is, keep it simple. The simpler and more focused your experiment the more likely it is to produce worthwhile results. No one method is better than any other but some methods are more relevant to your project than others. You will want the answers you find to be the most plausible answers to the question you have posed. To ensure this, have a clear, well-defined research question, remain focused on that question, and above all keep the experiment you design to collect your data simple.

Let us review. At its simplest, experimental research introduces an independent variable and measures the effect it has on a dependent variable. Can you identify the independent and dependent variables of your project? Look again at the activity in this chapter.

Here I would sound a note of caution, and perhaps we are jumping ahead a little to the results and discussion of your experiment. Be careful that, when you do an experiment where you have introduced and manipulated an independent variable to produce an effect on a dependent variable, you do not state that a cause and effect relationship exists when the results seen are influenced from outside. Always keep a critical eye.

Research Focus

It may be worth having a little break from your own study and considering a wider issue that is important in experimental research in sport.

Experimental research and sport

In many cases in sport there is debate on how research carried out addresses the *basic* versus *applied* question. This debate was highlighted earlier in this chapter. Another way of considering *basic* could be studies with high internal validity. These studies have high levels of control, but are so controlled they do not really reflect the real world of sport. Another way of considering *applied* are those studies with high external validity, which are open to the natural influences that are likely to be found in the real world of sport.

Atkinson and Neville (2001) examined this debate and noted that questions that can be answered through basic research, where that research is designed to corroborate or discount theories of the underlying mechanisms of a particular phenomenon, are often examined under very controlled conditions. Basic researchers may ask binary-type questions, those questions to which there are two answers, such as *Does variable x explain variable y, when all other variables are controlled?* It is the answer to such questions that help understanding of the processes involved in modelling physiological or psychological mechanisms. Theory-driven research questions like these can be addressed by classical hypothetico-deductive methods, the null hypothesis testing procedure and a sound researcher to be reasonably certain that, if all variables other than x have been controlled in an experiment, and the observed changes in y cannot be attributed to chance influences, then x must be the cause of y.

The cause and effect relationship

Applied researchers, on the other hand, may wish to investigate factors affecting variables in a more *real-world* setting. A more relevant question to the researcher working in an applied setting may be: *Does variable x, whatever the mechanism of its action, make a worthwhile difference to variable y in the real world?* In this research the cause and effect relationship may exist but the confidence that it exists is less because of all the confounding variables that may be present.

Experimental design

At the beginning of this chapter we used two examples to show how we could design an experiment when examining the experimental method. The next stage here is to decide on which is the best experimental design to use. What is the blueprint we will use to build our experimental method? It may seem that we have done things in the wrong order, we have got the bricks together before we know how to build the house but that is all right; the two actually need to work together. Because this chapter is about designing you should remember that it is fine to carry on refining your design until you are confident that it will yield the data, relatively free from error, that you can use to answer your question. Design modifications should stop though once you start to actually collect data; otherwise you will produce unreliable data.

Experimental design is simply how the manipulation and controlling of events and/or variables is achieved to answer a question or solve a problem. The goal of choosing a successful experimental research design is to allow you to conduct the study and test the hypothesis with a minimum of contamination from extraneous variables and error. This is an important point to remember as it has a dual element. It must allow you to conduct the study, but any design should be manageable by the researcher to allow research to be carried out in a timely fashion. The choice of research design that you choose may not be your first choice but must be one that allows the work to be completed whilst still maximising the potential effect. It should also allow testing of a hypothesis with a minimum of contamination from extraneous variables. Again, this may not always be possible to achieve and balancing these two issues is often a compromise. Simply, maximise the effect by minimising the threats. Keeping it simple will often help this be achieved.

Choosing an experimental design

There are many experimental designs to choose from. Some are off the shelf, some can be bespoke but they will fall into categories of true, quasi- and experimental design. How you select the design most appropriate for the research will depend upon answers to questions such as:

- the type of the research problem. Are you trying to establish a cause and effect or trying to explain a pre-existing relationship in a dependent variable?
- the number and variety of experimental variables. Are you manipulating the independent variable or creating variation in a dependent variable?
- how the groups will be formed. Is it random?
- whether you will be measuring the same participants on the same variable twice or more. This is known as repeated measures.
- what the threats to validity are that the research will attempt to control.

Poor experimental design will make all the effort and the whole research practice pointless. If you have a poorly thought through design that you then use to collect data you discover too late that the results are invalid. My advice is to run your research design past your peers and supervisor as they are likely to spot flaws that you may not. You can then act upon their feedback.

Once the questions above are satisfied what is needed is to determine the type of design that allows you to answer the question. Let's examine the research designs.

True experimental designs

If the experimental design used randomises its participants and has a control group, it is a true experimental design. However, the two true experimental designs often used are:

- post-test only design;
- pre- and post-test design.

Post-test only design

In its simplest form this design is where participants are randomly assigned to either the experimental or control group. Randomly assigning participants increases the chance of equivalence in the groups which is important as it is desirable to have two equivalent groups. The independent variable is introduced to the experimental group and testing is then carried out for the effects of the treatment on this group, with the same testing carried out on the control group to determine the effect of no treatment.

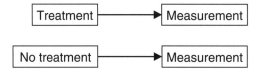

Figure 5.2 Post-test only design

In theory, assuming the two groups were equal at the beginning when the independent variable was given to the experimental group, any difference between the two groups at the end of the research is assumed to be due to the independent variable.

This design can be expanded to include more experimental groups if more than one level of independent variable is to be tested, and could also just have one group.

In the example of the training programmes, this is an excellent design. One group receives the training programme (treatment – measurement) the other group receives nothing but are the control, or comparison group. A drawback to this design is that you are not sure of the starting point of the groups. This is addressed by a pre- and post-test design.

Pre- and post-test design

The obvious difference between this design and the previous one is the inclusion of a pre-test. The inclusion of a pre-test has many advantages to the researcher. If the example of a post-test only design is used, one drawback is that it is difficult to determine exactly how much of any difference between the experimental group and the control group is due to the introduction of the independent variable. By pre-testing, the amount of change that is due to the introduction of the independent variable can be determined. Pre-testing also allows the two groups to be equivalent.

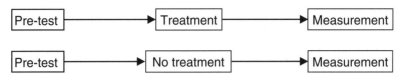

Figure 5.3 Pre- and post-test design

In the example of the training programmes, this is an even better design than the post-test only. One group still receives the training programme (treatment – measurement), the other group still receives nothing, being the control, or comparison group, but by pre-testing you are sure of the starting point of both groups and so effects can be more accurately measured. A drawback here is time. Measuring all the participants before allowing the treatment means allowing greater time for the study to be completed.

In both the post-test only and pre- and post-test designs a major factor to consider in your research project is the number of participants you will recruit. To ensure statistical power the groups should be reasonably large. This means recruiting a lot of participants, which is not always practical.

Quasi-experimental designs

The quasi-experimental designs are true experimental designs to a certain extent. Consequently the term *quasi* is used to indicate that they do not fully conform to the requirements of true experimental design. Often the factor that makes the design a quasi-experimental design is the inability of the researcher to randomly assign participants into groups. Because of this there will be doubt about the equivalence of groups. Some common quasi-experimental designs are:

- pre- and post-non-random design, or non-equivalent control groups;
- crossover design;
- time series.

Pre- and post-non-random design

This type of design has already been discussed but the reason it is considered quasi-experimental is that where participants are randomly assigned to either the experimental or control group in the true experimental designs, here they are not. Randomly assigning participants increases the chance of equivalence in the groups, which is important as it is normally desirable to have two equivalent groups. There are occasions where you will still have two groups but they will not be equivalent, such as if you were examining differences between genders or ages. A variation on the example of the training programme we have been using would be to look for differences in adaptation to training by a group of females against a group of males, or young against old.

Crossover design

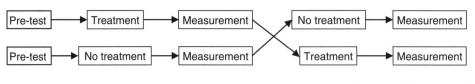

Figure 5.4 The crossover design

A crossover design is one that is very useful for some types of study, especially in sport. Its major benefit is that it requires only half the number of participants of a true experimental design; this is because the group acts as their own control group. Look at the design, it allows comparisons between two groups and there is a pre-test to ensure equivalence between groups. Then the groups swap and undergo the alternative, thereby acting as their own control.

The drawback here is that there needs to be a *wash out* period between swapping of the groups to allow any measured observed effects to be lost. In some cases the wash out period can be short, such as in some drug treatments, but in others the period is too long to be practical, as would be the case in our training programme example.

Time series

Figure 5.5 The time series

A time series design is an interesting design. Sometimes repeated measurements over time will help paint a more complete picture. Consider the example of psychological anxiety before a competition. By measuring anxiety a week before, a day before, an hour before, and then the same after the competition, a more complete picture of the development of anxiety can be painted. A series design is also the type of design that suits the examination of blood lactate levels with increasing treadmill speed.

Experimental designs

You should now understand better where your ideas for your own experiment and research design fit. When it can be logically determined that one factor produces a predictable influence on another, a cause and effect relationship is said to exist. The true experimental designs allow most control, so are more *basic* in the research continuum but allow higher confidence in establishing causality. Sometimes our research or other pressures such as time or availability of participants cause us to adopt a quasi-experimental research design. These types of design still allow quite a high level of control, and we can offer reasonable confidence in

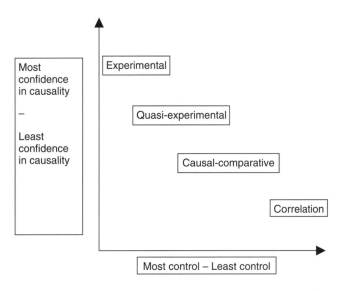

Figure 5.6 Experimental designs

establishing causality. As we progress to causal-comparative and correlation designs, we cannot be confident that causality exists. It may do, or we may just be observing a relationship that is not caused by one factor on another. Is the method you have chosen appropriate for the nature of your research and your research objectives?

I think my experiment is well designed, what do I do next?

One of the best things you can do is a pilot study. A pilot study allows you to make modifications to the methods and procedures to help reduce variability that will inevitably arise from things like biological variance, technician and equipment error and learning effect. A pilot study will help increase reliability and also provide an opportunity to record reliability of measurement techniques. To carry out a pilot study may seem time-consuming but the pay-off outweighs the cost. Include a pilot study in your research plan.

Chapter Review

The take-home messages from this chapter are:

• Experimental research can establish causality in experiments examining differences in groups. Whilst it can establish causality great care needs to be taken in how extraneous variables are controlled to ensure that no other influences are responsible for the effects you observe. Experimental research can also examine relationships between factors, although establishing the cause or mechanism behind that relationship is more complex.

- To understand experimental research you need to have a thorough understanding of the dependent and independent variables of your experiment.
- Maximise effect and minimise error by ensuring control in basic research. This may be more difficult in applied research where other influences are less controlled.
- The range of experimental designs offers a range of blueprint options for your experiment. When considering which one to use you need to think about whether it will maximise your predicted effect and also whether it is logistically possible to do, taking into consideration factors such as time and availability of participants.

Further Reading

Field, A (2003) *How to Design and Report Experiments*. London: Sage.

There are many texts that discuss experimental design. This is a particularly good one that I find very useful and applicable to many sport and exercise experiments.

Chapter 6
Non-experimental research

Learning Objectives

This chapter will help you to be able to:

- consider alternative methodologies to answer your research question;
- understand the concept of triangulation.

You will also be able to:

- consider using a mixed-method approach to your research project.

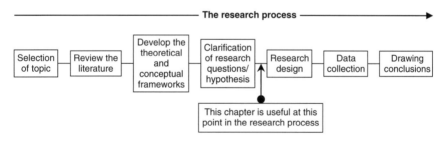

Figure 6.1 The research process: non-experimental research

Introduction

If you are considering an alternative method to collecting your data because the experimental approach does not seem to suit, then this chapter is for you. There are many topics in sport and exercise that would benefit from taking a non-experimental approach to researching them. You could also consider combining a non-experimental approach with an experimental one. This is known as mixed-methods research. Whatever the reason for considering a non-experimental approach to your research project, this chapter will help you understand some of the alternatives.

A non-experimental approach to researching a topic in sport and exercise can be a very worthwhile thing to do. Generally non-experimental methods are qualitative in nature. Understanding something in a qualitative way can give a very humanistic and detailed understanding of a topic, something which a quantitative approach can sometimes lack.

This chapter will examine qualitative approaches, such as observations, questionnaires and interviews. It will then discuss how data is collected with that approach, and give some ideas of how it could be used.

The non-experimental methods discussed can be used completely independently of other methods. However, when they are used in conjunction with other methods there is a possibility of using a method known as triangulation of data; this is discussed towards the end of the chapter. This chapter is not designed to be a comprehensive examination of qualitative research methods, but a brief overview that offers alternatives to an experimental approach. At the end of the chapter are a number of texts that I would recommend to learn more about qualitative methods of research.

What exactly is non-experimental research?

There will be times when manipulating an independent variable and therefore carrying out some type of experimental research is not possible. This may be because it is simply not possible, practical or possibly ethical to do so. This does not mean that there are not phenomena that are not worthy of investigation, and so research can still be carried out; it is just classified as non-experimental research. This technique of scientific enquiry can also be known as descriptive research, which is not to be confused with research with a descriptive purpose, as was highlighted in Chapter 2.

Let us examine some reasons why you may choose to do non-experimental research rather than experimental research. Sometimes you may not be able to replicate human behaviour in the laboratory and it is only clear in the field. An example of this would be observing acts of sportsmanship. In this example it is not possible to carry out experimental research, as creating incidents would not be representative of them actually occurring naturally. Alternatively, you may be interested in examining the use of steroids in body building and it would be unethical to use large doses, but you may find participants who do take large doses who you can observe naturally.

Non-experimental research studies still follow the basic elements of the scientific method. They may still have a hypothesis, which is clearly stated and tested, with conclusions drawn from the results. However, because this research is often carried out in a natural setting and you cannot control as many elements as you can in a laboratory, it is not as easy to establish a cause and effect relationship. In non-experimental research no independent variable is introduced and extraneous variables are difficult to control, and it is therefore difficult to conclude that variable A caused B to occur. This does not mean that logical deductions cannot be drawn about connections between variables. You may also be following a more inductive approach and so alternatives to experimental research are better approaches.

Examples of non-experimental research methods

Below follows a list of alternative research methods to experimental research. Each section will describe the method and the advantages and disadvantages using it can have; it will also describe ways of collecting data, general hints for carrying out the research and some examples of its use. It is not an exhaustive list but the methods presented are the most common non-experimental research methods in sport and exercise.

The methods are:

- observation studies;
- questionnaires;
- interviews;
- focus groups.

Observation studies

All good science includes elements of observation. Observation refers to the process of observing and recording events or situations. It should happen as much in experimental as non-experimental research. The technique is particularly useful for discovering whether individuals or groups do what they say they do, or behave in the way they say they do.

There are two main types of observation – participant and non-participant; non-participant observation is sometimes referred to as unobtrusive observation.

In participant observation the researcher becomes part of the group studied and participates in their daily life and activities, observing their everyday situations and their behaviour in these situations. Conversation is used in order to discover the participants' own interpretations of events.

In non-participant observation the researcher simply observes the activities without taking part themselves. Whilst this has the advantage of preventing the researcher from becoming involved in activities they may not wish to take part in, for example dangerous or criminal activities, they are less likely to understand fully the meanings behind behaviour in the group studied.

In observation studies the observer can remain covert, hiding their true identity as a researcher, or overt, where their identity is revealed to those studied. Overt or covert is different to participant or non-participant research as it is whether the participants can identify you as a researcher or not. It is argued that covert research will lead to a more valid study as the participants are less likely to change their behaviour if they do not know they are participating in research. However, the ethics of such studies should be questioned – have we the right to do this? In all research we have a responsibility to those being studied, that the research should not interfere with their physical, social or mental welfare. Because of these ethical considerations it is likely your institution will want to ensure all safeguards are taken when carrying out covert observations.

The advantage to observing is that to carry it out requires little training or familiarisation. You can begin to understand the meanings behind the actions you see and the behaviour you witness is seen in its natural environment with the participant undisturbed. Observing can be very flexible and may expose phenomena not before seen, particularly in groups where little is known.

There are some disadvantages to observing as a non-experimental method, and they include the time it takes to observe and the problems you may have in recording accurately and reliably what you see. It is likely you will only be able to observe a small group and there are also likely to be limitations to your ability to generalise from that group. There are also ethical, moral and perhaps even legal issues to consider, especially when observing deviant groups, such as football hooligans, or when the observation is covert.

Data collection

It is impossible to keep a record of everything and you must decide at the outset where your interests lie. You may decide to film or tape record events, although the cost of this may be quite substantial. Data is often recorded through writing up notes in private after the event or you could set up your own complex system with specific categories of behaviour for post-observation recordings using graphs, charts and plans. These will vary depending on the specific problem under investigation; there is no one perfect example which can be used in all situations.

What is important is careful preparation before observation begins; remember the aim of observation is to be unobtrusive so that behaviour remains as normal as possible. Placing a tape recorder under someone's nose or scribbling down notes in front of them will not help to maintain this. There are disadvantages with this method of gathering data. The most common criticism is that it is highly subjective, dependent in large part on the researcher's own focus and ideas of what should be recorded and their own interpretations of what they have observed.

General ideas for carrying out observation

This is not an easy option for a research project but a method which takes meticulous planning. You should enter the field with a clear idea of exactly what it is you wish to discover or vast amounts of time and effort can be wasted. An example of the use of participant observation could be in studies of the social structure and functioning of small communities or deviant groups, such as football hooligans.

Questionnaires

A questionnaire is a type of survey where respondents write answers to questions posed by the researcher on a question form. A number of respondents are asked identical questions in order to gain information that can be analysed, patterns found and comparisons made.

Questionnaires are extremely flexible and can be used to gather information on almost any topic involving large or small numbers of people. The commonest type of questionnaire involves closed choice or fixed questions where the respondent is required to answer by choosing an option from a number of given answers, usually by ticking a box or circling an answer. These types of questionnaires only gather straightforward, uncomplicated information, and simple questions only can be asked. The open-ended questionnaire differs in that it allows the respondent to formulate and record their answers in their own words. These are more qualitative and can produce detailed answers to complex problems.

Example: closed choice question

People go to the recreation centre for different reasons; for which of the following four reasons do you most go?

- to work out or train;
- to play competitive sport;
- to meet friends or socialise;
- to participate in a non-sporting activity, such as a crèche.

Example: open-ended question

People go to the recreation centre for different reasons; for what reason do you most go?

There are advantages and disadvantages associated with each method. Open-ended questions give a greater insight and understanding of the topic researched but may be difficult to classify and quantify and must be carefully interpreted. Closed choice questions are easy to classify and quantify, require less time, effort and ingenuity, but do not allow the respondents to qualify, develop or clarify their answers.

Using questionnaires to gather data has some very important advantages, such as, it is generally a very quick, efficient and cheap way to reach a large number of people. The consistent form of the way the questions are presented helps eliminate bias that could be introduced by the researcher. There are some general disadvantages too: many forms of questionnaire will only allow a limited answer to be given. Even though you are able to explore qualitatively there is often no way to probe some of the answers more deeply; this can result in superficial responses. There are also problems in the way the questionnaire is administered: some methods result in low response rates, the construction of the questionnaire is difficult, and checking and verifying the accuracy of the answers is difficult as questions will often mean different things to different people.

Data collection

The information required will be recorded on the form itself by the respondent. Questionnaires can be given to the respondent personally and completed on the spot, or can be posted which, although much quicker, increases the cost and decreases the response rate and hence representativeness. Web-based questionnaires are often seen as easy to respond to by survey participants.

General ideas for constructing questionnaires

Get the beginning right, this will encourage respondents to read on. It should state what the survey is about and roughly how long it will take to complete. Make the questionnaire look attractive – use space well and avoid a cramped appearance. Use a large enough type size and avoid block capitals so that questions can be easily read. Keep sentences short and sentence construction simple, the wording of the questionnaire is all important. Avoid leading questions which direct the respondent in a particular way, for example, *Isn't it true to say that.* . . . Avoid jargon and technical terms, and make sure the question is not ambiguous – each question should only lead to one interpretation. Watch out for double questions – that is, asking two separate questions at once. An example of the use of questionnaires would be when the researcher wants to gather data from a scattered population. More information about questionnaires can be found in the recommended resources at the end of this section.

Interviews

Interviews are a type of survey where questions are delivered in a face-to-face encounter by an interviewer. An interview is much like a conversation except there is a specific purpose to it. It has the purpose of obtaining information relevant to a particular research topic. It is initiated by the researcher and is focused on specific content.

As with questionnaires, interviews can be approached from either a quantitative or qualitative angle and there are many variations on the general method. Purely quantitative interviews are rather like a closed ended questionnaire that the interviewer fills in for the respondent. These are highly structured, formal interviews which are determined in advance and have fixed responses.

At the other end of the scale, the unstructured, purely qualitative interview is rather like an informal conversation. Here questions are asked in the natural course of interaction and arise from the particular context.

A large number of interviews will fall somewhere in between these two extremes and are known as semi-structured interviews. These have specific questions already predetermined that are asked to the respondent in a particular order, or topics and issues to be covered in the course of the interview.

There are advantages and disadvantages associated with each type of method. Structured interviews maximise reliability and are easier to classify and quantify. By contrast unstructured interviews can give a greater insight and more in-depth understanding of the topic researched, but need more expertise to control and more time for analysis.

Interviews have distinct advantages to other methods in that you generally will get a higher response rate to being interviewed than asking people to fill in a questionnaire. Interviews also can give an opportunity to gather complex information in a relaxed environment, where the researcher has a high degree of control. Some disadvantages are that they can be difficult to analyse, very time consuming and limited to a small sample. Also, interviews are open to interviewer bias and this needs to be addressed. Occasionally you may also get a hostile reaction.

Data collection

A structured format can leave the interviewer with the job of simply ticking a number of boxes on a form. A less structured format necessitates a different technique for recording data. A tape recorder is often used to collect information in an unstructured interview. This has the advantage over note taking in that everything will have been recorded, details cannot be missed, and the interviewer can give their full attention to the respondent. However, the interviewee may be uncomfortable knowing they are on tape. Alongside this, transcribing the tapes is a very time consuming process; this is something to bear in mind if embarking on this method of data collection for your research project.

General ideas for carrying out interviews

Begin with an explanation of who you are and what the survey is about, and assure confidentiality. Try to achieve rapport with the respondent: be friendly and look as if you are enjoying the interview and are interested in what they have to say. Be aware of the importance of body language in face-to-face interviews. Research has shown that interviewees are more at ease with someone who is similar to them in terms of ethnicity, class, sex, speech and dress code. Whilst the majority of these cannot be changed, you can dress in a similar manner to your interviewee; if interviewing a company director at their place of work they are unlikely to be wearing jeans and a T-shirt, a suit would be more suitable. Be familiar with your questions and ask them in a neutral manner; try not to lead respondents to answer in a certain way. Be aware of your role as an interviewer, which is to listen, not to speak. Take a full record of the interview either through tape recording or note taking. Prompts may be necessary if information is not given freely. An example of the usefulness of an interview is when a researcher aims to discover detailed answers to complex questions in a face-to-face situation. The respondents can give quite elaborate answers, for example, opinion polls, life histories.

Focus groups

The focus group is a type of interview that involves carefully selected individuals who usually do not know each other. They generally consist of seven to ten members as well as the researcher. These individuals are selected as they hold particular characteristics which the researcher believes are necessary to the topic of focus. A group discussion is held in a permissive environment in order to extract opinions and share ideas and perceptions through group interaction. It is not necessary to reach a consensus.

Focus groups are extremely useful in providing qualitative data which give an insight into attitudes and perceptions difficult to obtain using other procedures. The interviewer acts as a moderator and listener posing predetermined open-ended questions which the respondents answer in any way they choose.

Learning Activity 6.1

The chapter so far has given a brief overview of some of the more popular non-experimental methods that are commonly used in sport and exercise research. It is not an exhaustive overview and you should use the further reading to guide you.

- Think about the difference between quantitative and qualitative research methods and think of where examples of each could be used in your research project.
- Go back and read again the examples of particular non-experimental research methods to discover which will be the most useful for your particular research project, weighing up the advantages and disadvantages of each.
- Carry out some further reading about methods you believe to be appropriate for you.

Triangulation of data

When you are collecting data you may find that using only one method of data collection may not offer enough evidence to substantiate an answer to your initial question, or you may want to consolidate what you think you have found with another method of data collection. Triangulation of data refers to using multiple methods of data collection to examine one phenomenon. Consider physical activity in school. You may approach this subject using only an observational approach, but by also including a carefully designed questionnaire and using some interviews, you can examine this topic in much more depth. This combination of methods will help confirm or deny what you may only find in one approach. Using one method alone means you may miss the *truth*; another method will help locate it more accurately, but using three helps to triangulate the *truth* much more effectively.

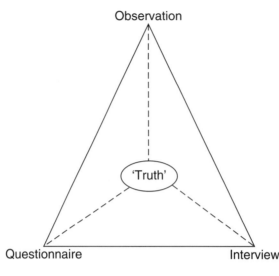

Figure 6.2 The triangulation of data

Causal relationships and a word of warning

The methods described in this chapter do offer many advantages over using an experimental method. They can be more humanistic, descriptive and can reveal the *why* more than the *what*. On discovering the *what* it can be very tempting to make the leap to conclude a causation. Here we must differentiate between a causal relationship and a cause and effect relationship. A causal relationship is different to a cause and effect relationship. A causal relationship is where variables that are observed appear to have a connection and this connection may be demonstrated mathematically by using a correlation; however the connection that appears to be there is neither known nor explained. It is really important to note that I have used the words *may* a lot here and this is deliberate. Even though statistics may show a relationship through a correlation, it does not mean that one exists and so it is vital that you are cautious in suggesting causal relationships. An example I like to give to my classes is that there is a relationship in arm length and leg length in children. This can be shown by a very strong positive correlation that if both are measured over a period of years as one gets longer so does the other. This does not mean though that growth in my leg length causes growth in my arm length. An example of a cause and effect relationship is students not handing in assignments not receiving a grade. The cause is the not handing in, the effect is not receiving a grade.

Chapter Review

The take-home messages from this chapter are:

- Non-experimental methods of research offer a viable alternative to experimental methods in some cases of research in sport and exercise. The choice is often determined by the research question you have developed and then by personal preference.

- Non-experimental methods of research can be used alongside experimental methods in a mixed-method design. If you consider quantitative methods to examine the *what* in something you observe, the qualitative methodology can provide the *why* it is happening. Again some research questions may just require a what or a why approach, but to combine them is sometimes worthwhile for a more comprehensive approach.
- This is not an exhaustive description of the range of possible methods, but just a few of the popular approaches. In the further reading below are a number of texts I would recommend in order to be able to understand this approach more thoroughly.

Further Reading

These texts are specific sport and exercise texts which cover in more detail the methods I have discussed. They will provide a very useful guide as to how the specific research approach can be made.

- Gratton, C and Jones, I (2003) *Research Methods for Sport Studies.* London: Routledge.
- Long, J (2007) *Researching Leisure, Sport and Tourism. The essential guide.* London: Sage.
- Berg, K (2004) *Essentials of Research Methods in Health, Physical Education, Exercise Science and Recreation.* Second edition. Baltimore: Lippincott Williams and Wilkins.
- Andrews, D (2005) *Qualitative Methods in Sports Studies.* New York: Berg.
- Tenenbaum, G (2005) *Methods of Research in Sport Sciences. Quantitative and qualitative approaches.* Oxford: Meyer and Meyer Sport.

Chapter 7
Writing the why

Learning Objectives

This chapter will help you to be able to:

- understand the format and structure of your research report;
- understand the conventions of scientific writing;
- consider the likely audience of your research report and adjust your writing style to suit that audience.

You will also be able to:

- write an initial draft of your introduction and literature review.

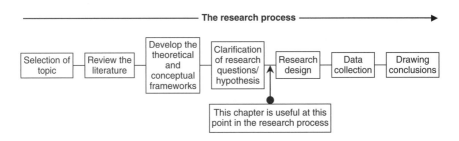

Figure 7.1 The research process: writing the why

Introduction

This chapter is essential for everyone who has to present a finished research project. Presenting your work is the culmination of your research project and to ensure that credit is given it is essential that the quality of that presentation reflects the quality of the research project itself. This chapter is the first of four chapters that break up the writing of your research project into manageable sections. By the end of each chapter you will be able to write first drafts of the sections that chapter covers.

- *Writing the why* will cover the introduction and literature review;
- *Writing the how* will cover the method;
- *Writing what you have found* will cover the results;
- *Writing the so what* will cover the discussion and conclusion.

If you are presenting your research project in a different format to a conventional written report, such as a poster, there are still some important aspects that are common to scientific presentation, so it is still essential reading.

Key to any research project is the ability to clearly communicate its findings to the intended audience. It may be that for your first research project that audience may only be your institution's academic staff, it may be that you intend to publish your findings to a wider audience, but the quality of your communication must match the quality of your research project.

This chapter is designed to help you begin to transfer the work and research that you have done so far into the beginnings of a well-structured and well-presented report. This is particularly important as most research projects are generally some of the biggest pieces of academic work you will ever do, and writing them up can be a very onerous task, especially if left till towards the end. It is vital that your research report communicates what you have done, why you have done it and what you have found.

In order to do your research justice and to get a good mark it is essential that you produce an integrated and cohesive report that documents your research in a concise and objective manner. It will also need to be well presented as most examiners are put off by poorly laid-out and badly proofread documents. Starting this work now gives you time to achieve this and remain sane.

This chapter begins by establishing some common threads about your research report. It will discuss how to write to make it count, ensuring you keep a structure and common thread throughout the report. Some of the common formatting issues are examined and tips on how to make formatting easier are also presented. Guidance is also given on how to write a coherent introduction and literature review, with many of the potential pitfalls and common mistakes highlighted. At this point in the research project you should be able to draft an initial introduction and literature review.

Write to make it count

Writing in science is about communicating. When presenting your research project you are communicating your findings to your peers for them to consider and critically evaluate. If this is your first research project your aim may be different to this. It is likely you are writing to communicate your findings not to your peers but to be critically considered by your tutor, supervisor or the final assessor of your work. However, they will often wear two hats when considering your work, one as an academic, so they will look for evidence of your learning and understanding, but also one as a fellow researcher, so they will look for evidence of good research practice. So as you write you need to consider how to show you have learned through carrying out the process and also how you have carried out sound scientific practice, because ultimately your work will be assessed and you want to ensure that every word you write counts in that assessment.

To help make sure your research project counts when you present your findings, bear two things in mind. Firstly, your report needs to present your research accurately, usually starting with the research objectives and the literature review and finishing with conclusions about your results in terms of these objectives and the existing literature. This *circular thread* or story that will run throughout your project report will ensure that your research is presented as an integrated whole.

As we are only considering writing the initial drafts of the introduction and literature review this *circular thread* may not be fully established or even understood yet, but you should realise that it is there, and

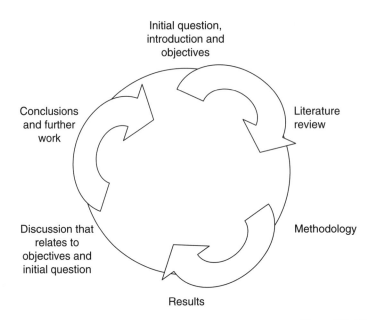

Figure 7.2 The circular thread

be prepared to go back to these initial sections over and over again, polishing them and integrating them as the other aspects are written and contribute to the whole picture. The four chapters about how to write the report will help in this aspect.

Secondly, does your work look good? You may think that this is a secondary issue and perhaps a minor point, but not only is a well-presented report easier to read, it also communicates the essence of your research findings more effectively. Poorly structured, misspelt, badly organised reports make it harder for the reader to work out the message that you are actually trying to get over. They obscure and therefore diminish the impact of your findings and all that hard work. Producing well-presented work also demonstrates that you have been able to manage the research process sufficiently well to ensure that you have time to take care over the presentation of the end result. A simple experiment to demonstrate this is to compare how you feel reading a well-presented report and a not so well-presented report. One report makes things clear and easy to understand; the other will frustrate and confuse you. Personally as a tutor, I would also tend to think that if the final report is sloppy then perhaps the research behind it may be too. Remember, write to make it count.

Before we go any further in examining writing generally, it is vital that you ensure that you are meeting the requirements of your institution. Your institution always has the final say in how your research project should be presented, so consult your academic handbooks, supervisor or tutor, and consider these points.

- Are you clear on what is required of you and what help you can get?
- Are there written guidelines you can refer to on what is required when presenting your research project?
- Can you consult good examples produced by previous students? If you do this, remember that they may not be working to the same criteria as you.
- Do you understand what you are aiming to achieve in writing your report? Use this chapter to help and also consider asking your supervisor to clarify it for you.

The key to producing a successful research project and report, from the conception through to the final dissemination of the findings, is the ability to multi-task throughout. To work on different tasks as you progress helps achieve your aim, particularly as it is likely you have a tight deadline to meet. You might think the writing only occurs once all the data is collected, and whilst the final draft of the whole report can only be produced then, there is nothing to stop you getting a head start and beginning to draft out sections as you go along.

Consider that whenever and whatever you write there are a number of things that you should consider to ensure your communication is effective at conveying the message you want to. In presenting your research project you are aiming to develop a concise report that conveys your findings clearly and unambiguously. Achieving this is an art form in itself and this chapter will help you in achieving this, but one thing that is vital is to make sure that you write the report for the intended audience.

The audience

The first question you should answer is, *Who is going to read the report?* Reports will differ considerably depending on whether the audience will want or require technical detail, whether they are looking for a summary of results, or whether they are about to examine your research in a Ph.D. exam. Consider some of the research articles you have already read; did the authors of those consider you when they were writing them? If the report was structured in such a way that it led you through each part, it was easily understood, and the results were easy to understand, then it is likely the author did consider you. If you found some reports poorly structured or written, overly technical or just plainly confusing then it is likely they did not consider you. It is difficult to consider the exact audience of your report because you can never really be sure of their motives for reading the research, but you must aim to communicate with clarity. However, if this is your first major research project you have a major advantage in that you are likely to know personally the audience of your research report; when you write, keep this audience in mind.

Case Study

Andy, a student who has recently finished a research project that examined the bio-mechanics of climbing techniques, told me:

> *When I started my project I was constantly trying to explain what I was doing to anyone who would listen. This really helped me write things like the introduction because the more times I explained it the clearer it became to me.*

Something I felt Andy was achieving here was that written communication is easier when you imagine that you are trying to explain it to someone who is interested and intelligent but not necessarily familiar with what you are doing. Try telling an imaginary audience.

The story

Earlier I suggested that a research report should have a circular thread to it. You can consider this thread to be the story of your research project, or the path you will take the reader of your report down. You might not think that scientific writing should have a story but it does; it is not, however, the story of what you did but more about why and how you did it, and then what you found and what that means. You lead the reader through each stage helping them understand why you have done what you have done, as well as explaining what you found.

The central theme of the story is likely to centre on a specific research finding, or perhaps a methodological problem or challenge. When you write your report, you should attempt to tell the story to your reader. Even in very formal journal articles where you will be required to be concise and detailed at the same time, a good storyline can help make an otherwise very dull report interesting to the reader, because ultimately you are writing for them and with them in mind.

The hardest part of telling the story in your research is finding the story you want to tell in the first place. You have already achieved this. Chapters 2 and 3 identified the central plot and main characters when you started to develop your research question. As time has progressed the story has become clearer for you in your own mind. By the time you come to be able to write at least the first drafts of your story, you will have been steeped in the detail of the story for weeks or months, possibly years. Remember, you were warned; research can be a big part of your life.

Even though you are immersed in your research project it is important to look up from it once in a while. To find the story in your research, you have to look at the big picture and remember what the story is that you are trying to tell. You have to try to view your research from your audience's perspective. You may have to let go of some of the details that you obsessed so much about and leave that minutiae out of the write-up or move them to technical appendices or tables where they will not cloud the story for your audience. Concentrate on helping your audience to understand your ideas. Convince the audience of your research project through your story.

Formatting considerations

One thing which is very important to get right, but which is relatively easy to accomplish, is the formatting of the report. You must find out what the formatting requirements of your institution are. To ignore them or not fully follow the requirements will inevitably lead to very easy marks being lost. In the future, if you continue to be a researcher, it is important to know and understand what the specific formatting considerations are, as each journal or source that you may submit research to will ask you to follow specific formatting guidelines. Every institution I know of has very strict policies about formatting and style. What are your institution's?

The format of the report

The report as a whole is likely to have the following structure:

- title page;
- abstract;
- introduction;
- literature review;

- methods;
- results;
- discussion and conclusions;
- references;
- appendices.

With an overall structure you can consider creating a template on your word processor. It is vital you fully utilise the word processing package you are using. It is one of the most powerful tools that you will use, and you are probably not using it as effectively as you could. One thing you can easily do is create a template that meets the formatting requirements and write up all your work on that. Then you can be confident that you are meeting those requirements.

Formatting within the report

To illustrate what the formatting within the structure of a research report might require, consider the bullet points below. You must check these against the specific formatting guidelines not only for your institution but also for the type of report you are writing. The details below are general for a scientific report but your research may not be required to be presented in this way. Try to view samples of previous work from your institution but also remember that that work may itself not meet the formatting guidelines, or they may have changed since it was originally written. Formatting requirements include:

- sizes of page margins and line spacing;
- formats of the title page, the contents list, appendices, the reference list, illustrations, figures and tables;
- numbering systems for chapters and sections, pages, figure and table captions, equations;
- font-styles for chapter and section headings, other text, figure and table captions, equations, and quoted work;
- how references are cited;
- how tables, figures and equations are cited;
- whether the publication should be written in a particular tense or person.

Typically, the layout of a page should be as follows:

- left margin: 40mm;
- top, bottom and right margins: 25mm;
- text font: 12 point Times Roman or Times New Roman;
- line spacing: 1.5 lines.

Learning Activity 7.1

Now that you understand the overall structure and format the report should follow, as an activity create a word processing template that meets those requirements.

Scientific writing

Within the style of writing the research report there needs to be consideration of the scientific conventions. Generally first person and sex-stereotyped forms are avoided. Material should be presented in an unbiased and unemotional manner. For example, no statements about your feelings should be included. This does not necessarily mean the material should be presented in an uninteresting fashion. This can be hard to achieve at times, but remember that research is objective and not subjective. It is likely with practice you will develop a number of ways to reword something in a scientific way, rather than the way you would normally say it.

Also consider parallel construction: this is where the tense you use, whether present, past or future, is kept parallel within and between sentences that you write. The use of tense is important. Using the past tense to quote the work of others is always preferred. Look at your sentence structure and ensure your punctuation is correct. Incomplete and run-on sentences should be avoided. Word processors will often flag sentence structure and grammatical errors in green to alert you. If it does flag an error, try to re-structure it. Nothing can infuriate a reader more – sometimes so much they concentrate on it more than the research itself – than poor spelling and inappropriate word usage. You must ensure your spelling is correct and use of words is appropriate and that words are capitalised and abbreviated correctly. Just because a red line does not appear underneath it on your screen does not mean the word is correct; always proofread and get a friend or peer to proofread for you. Something I am very aware of when writing documents is how sometimes the word processing package can result in using a mixture of dictionaries. If you are writing in English your word processing package will be able to spell words using both UK and US spellings. It is both annoying and slightly suspicious when you read a document that mixes spelling from both dictionaries. For example, the words *generalise* and *generalize* might appear in the same document. Use one dictionary, preferably the one of your country, and stick with it throughout the document. The general style and outcome should be that the document you produce is neat and reads well, and that the required format for the document has been correctly followed. With these general considerations of scientific writing completed we can examine how to write an introduction and literature review.

Writing the why

When we refer to writing the why, we mean writing the initial part of the report, the introduction section and the literature review, the part designed to explain to the reader why you are doing what you are doing. Although there are other parts of the report that come before the introduction and literature review they are normally written at the end, such as the abstract, or play no part in telling the story, such as the title page and contents page, so they do not need to be considered here.

The purpose of the introduction is to help the reader understand what the rationale or justification is for your particular research project, help them understand some of the background behind it and to set the scene for the coming story. It should introduce the research by situating it, giving it background, presenting the research problem and saying how and why this problem will be solved. Without this important information the reader cannot easily understand the more detailed information about the research project as they have no context for it. It also explains why the research is being done, the rationale for the research, which is crucial for the reader to understand fully the significance of the study. A critical reader will always say, *so what?*, and you need to answer this question for them.

You can break the introduction down into three parts, in which each section will increase in specificity as you go through it.

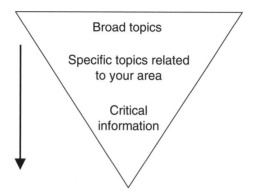

Broad topics

Specific topics related
to your area

Critical
information

Figure 7.3 Breaking the introduction down

The first level explains to the reader what the problems and issues are in this particular area of research. This sets the scene and gives context. The second level then explains your own research project, without too much detail, how it is addressing some of those problems, and how it will contribute to scientific knowledge and understanding. The third level will consider some of the outcomes of your research and, if applicable, make specific predictions.

Setting the scene

Your research project has come to the point that it is at now through your own ideas but has gained those ideas through the research of previous findings or theoretical ideas. It is vital that you allow the reader to understand, quickly and briefly, how you came to your own ideas through consideration of that research.

In setting the scene you need to provide background information about relevant and previous research. It is best to keep it confined to directly relevant material, and keep it focused on your research. A common mistake is to use this part to explain everything. This is not only wasteful but very off-putting to the reader. Make some assumptions here that the reader of your research is intelligent and informed but still needs to understand the specific topic area and the research behind it; in short consider the saying, *do not teach your granny to suck eggs*. What you are attempting to do is make a statement of constructs, where each key construct in the research project is explained and the explanations are readily understandable to an intelligent reader.

You then want to clearly and unambiguously state the problem you are investigating. You may consider it appropriate to your research to also give a statement of a causal relationship where you relate the cause–effect relationship to be studied to the problem area.

The second part of the introduction will then go on to explain your own study and what you intend to do. Clearly and briefly explain how it addresses some of those problems you have already highlighted and how it will contribute to scientific knowledge and understanding. If there is a gap in the literature, here is the time to highlight it. This section should tease the reader with enough detail to help them see the bigger picture, not so much to put them off. You are creating interest for them to delve deeper into your report where the actual detail is.

The third part will consider some of the outcomes of your research and if applicable make specific predictions. It may be appropriate and required by your institution to make a statement of the hypothesis; by now of course the relationship of the hypothesis to both the problem statement and relevant research should be readily understood. If it is not, then it still needs some work. Always consider your audience.

Use these questions as prompts to help you write the introduction section.

- What is the context of this problem? In what situation or environment can this problem be observed? This is the background.
- Why is this research important? Who will benefit? Why do we need to know this? Why does this situation, method, model or piece of equipment need to be improved? This is the rationale.
- What is it we do not know? What is the gap in our knowledge this research will fill? What needs to be improved? This is the problem statement.
- What steps will you the researcher take to try and fill this gap or improve the situation? These are the objectives.
- What are the limitations to the research? Is there any aspect of the problem the research will not discuss? Is the study limited to a specific population or only to certain aspects of the situation? This is the scope.
- What limitations are set upon the researcher? Is there any factor, condition or circumstance that prevents the researcher from achieving all his/her objectives? These are the delimitations.
- What are the expected assumptions? In considering the method, model, formulation or approach, does the research take certain conditions, states, or requirements for granted? Are there certain fundamental conditions or states the researcher takes to be true? These are the assumptions.

Writing is a very structured process and a useful way to think about it is as being like a Russian doll. You can open up a Russian doll and find a smaller doll inside, over and over again. Writing is similar. The overall section needs a funnel-like structure; inside this funnel are the paragraphs that also have a funnel structure, all stacking within this overall section.

Common problems seen in an introduction

Here are a number of common problems seen in an introduction.

Too much detail

Sometimes I read introductions that have too much detail and hence are too long. Remember, this is the *introduction*, a kind of overview. Although you will cover important points, detailed descriptions of methodology and results will be in later sections. Look at the proportion of a research paper an introduction takes up. Notice that it is comparatively short because it serves as a *summary* of what follows. Ensure you do not try to cover everything, remember, be brief and to the point.

Repetition of words, phrases or ideas

You will have key words that are crucial to your study. However, your reader does not want to read them over and over again. A high level of repetition makes your writing look careless. To reduce it, highlight repeated words or phrases; you can then easily judge if you are overusing them by visually noticing how often they appear and find synonyms or pronouns to replace them.

Unclear problem definition

Without a clear definition of your research problem, your reader is left with no clear idea of what you were studying. This means that they cannot judge the relevance of your work to their own work, or its usefulness, quality, etc. Remember, we write to make it count. As an exercise, you should be able to complete a sentence that starts, *The purpose of this study is . . .* , that concisely encapsulates the problem you are investigating. This is a good exercise but do not include this exact sentence in your research report. It serves as an easy way to check that you have a clearly defined problem. In your research report you should be able to write your research problem in one sentence; you can add details in the sentences that follow. You should also ensure that your research problem matches the title of your report – you would be surprised how many do not – as well as its methodology and objectives.

Poor organisation

Writing an introduction that effectively introduces your research problem and encapsulates your study is not an easy task. Often when we write we discover gradually what we want to say and how we want to say it. Writing is often a process of discovery and that is another good reason for starting it early. Bear this in mind when you write your introduction, and be prepared to go back and make big changes to what you have written, and the order in which you have presented your ideas and information. Your introduction must have a logical sequence that your reader can follow easily.

Writing the literature review

Chapter 4 discussed the literature review – where to find and how to assess the literature – and it suggested some things to consider when starting drafting the literature review. Like any major essay, the literature review needs to be planned, drafted and re-drafted until you are happy with it. Do not consider it finished until the end of the research project though, because undoubtedly you will still be gathering, reading and assessing literature that can contribute to it. Consider the circular thread idea. As you build your discussion, you are sure to link back to your literature review and you are likely to revise both sections.

This part of the chapter will examine how to structure your literature review, how to ensure it relates to your research question, give some tips and hints on writing it, and highlight common mistakes that occur.

Before you start to write the literature review consider its purpose. We are writing to make it count and to make this section count, your literature review will need to demonstrate to the reader your familiarity with and knowledge of the subject area of which your research project is a part. It is also there to provide an outline of the relevant theories and concepts important within your research project. I use a mind map to help organise the literature review into different sections.

With any essay, which is essentially what a literature review is, there needs to be a structure underlying it. The easiest structure to follow, and which will work in every section, is to introduce the topic, providing a context and then go onto the main body of that work.

Once again start with a broad overview of relevant ideas, concepts and definitions and then work towards the more specific. How you decide to group the areas underneath that is a matter of choice and sometimes necessity; you could for example group together research that has examined similar problems or used similar methodologies. In some cases, it can also be approached in a historical order. However you do it, ensure that the main contributions in the review come from research that is most relevant. Other research may be interesting but that does not necessarily make it relevant; we are writing to make it count.

With your literature review it is vital that you relate the writing you produce to the research question that you are working on. Guide the reader in understanding how the research you are reviewing has contributed to your research thinking. Do not be overly explicit. You must always be objective and allow the reader to draw their own conclusions but by the structure and emphasis you place on things within the review, the reader should reach similar thoughts as your own.

Common mistakes in literature reviews

It is very unlikely you will get your literature review written to your satisfaction on the first attempt. It is a piece of work that needs to be crafted, polished and only then presented. There are some common mistakes that should be avoided at all costs.

- The review is simply a list of past studies that are merely described.
- The literature does not relate to the study at hand.
- The literature review has not taken time to identify and highlight the most relevant and important work.
- The literature review has not appreciated the relevant wider sources and topics.
- The review has not used primary sources but has relied too much upon secondary sources of literature.
- The review has not critically examined the literature.
- The review has not considered the contrary findings and alternative explanations.
- The review has not addressed problematic issues that have arisen.

Start to write

Now start to write! It can be daunting to try and convert the mass of information that you have gathered up to this point, and in the same way that the initial part of developing your study seemed confusing at times so will writing it. The only way to clear that confusion is to start to write it out. Consider the process of getting the words onto the page as being the same as laying out building blocks. Building the introduction or the literature review is then only a matter of moving the blocks into place.

One of the major problems that you will face when carrying out a research project is underestimating how difficult it is, and how long it takes to write up research. If you do not know how to start, plan it out, perhaps in a mind map, and then start to write. Set small manageable targets, perhaps 500 words, and give yourself rewards. Anything that will get you into the process of writing is good and it should become easier from there.

Writing the introduction and literature review: a checklist

- Have you set yourself deadlines and kept to them?
- Do you write regularly?
- When you have completed your reading for one section of the literature review do you write it up?
- Do you check that you have covered all essential requirements of the introduction and literature review?
- Are you taking care to stay within the required word limit and your targeted limit for that section?
- Is the structure of your report simple and easy to follow? Use subheadings to structure individual sections.
- Think carefully about how you will ensure that the introduction and literature review link together. The use of subheadings that relate to each other may help you to avoid the trap of losing the focus of your research.
- Number tables and figures and provide titles.
- Check your referencing system is correct for your institution. Make sure you have acknowledged your sources.
- Check your bibliography for errors.
- Have you given yourself enough time to revise your writing and asked someone to proofread it for mistakes in grammar, paragraph structure, spelling and understanding?
- Have you avoided using jargon and technical language as much as possible? Where it is used, explain its meaning to the reader.
- Check that you have stated the aims of the research clearly.
- Remember to see your supervisor regularly for help and guidance.
- *Do not* give up – most people find it difficult to write, even those who write for a living.

Chapter Review

The take-home messages from this chapter are:

- You need to understand the conventions of scientific writing. It will save you time if you can attempt to write your first drafts in the required conventions, rather than attempt to correct it once it is done.

- Consider the structure, both of the overall section and of the paragraph that you are writing. When you write to make it count you are not only writing concisely and clearly but also writing to lead the reader down the same pathway as you. A funnel-type structure helps achieve that.
- Be aware of the potential pitfalls of writing an introduction or literature review. Use the advice of this book and the comments from your supervisor or lecturer to avoid the common mistakes that we have seen in many research reports.
- Start to write. It may seem daunting when the report you have to produce has a targeted word limit of thousands of words, but every journey begins with the first step. The first step for you to get the work you have completed in a presentable form of communication is to write.

Further Reading

In previous chapters I have highlighted many key texts that are specific to sport and exercise and that I consider excellent relevant help to that particular chapter. Most of those texts will have useful guidance on how to write an introduction or literature review.

For these chapters on writing I am going to suggest a range of books that provide excellent guidance for writing in general. These include both texts for writing specifically and texts for study skills that will include help in writing.

- Pritchard, A (2008) *Studying and Learning at University. Vital skills for success in your degree.* London: Sage.
- Barrass, R (2002) *Scientists Must Write.* Second edition. London: Routledge.
- Burns, T and Sinfield, S (2008) *Essential Study Skills. The complete guide to success at university.* Second edition. London: Sage.
- Turk, C (2001) *Effective Writing. Improving scientific, technical and business communication.* Second edition. London: Spon Press.
- Johnson, W (2007) *Write to the Top.* New York: Palgrave Macmillan.
- O'Connor, M (1999) *Writing Successfully in Science.* London: E & F N Spon.

Part 2
You're off

Chapter 8
You're off: making ethics applications

This is the second part of this book and is entitled *You're off* because it is from this point that the practicalities of a research project really kick in. Up to this point it has really been about thinking and planning the project, but you should now be in a position to start to collect data and to see those plans through. The first part of this section is about making ethics applications. This is a necessary first step to collecting data.

Learning Objectives

This chapter will help you to be able to:

- consider the ethical integrity of your own research project;
- deliberate on some of the ethical considerations that are needed when carrying out your research project.

You will also be able to:

- compile an ethics application for your institution;
- complete an informed consent form for your research project.

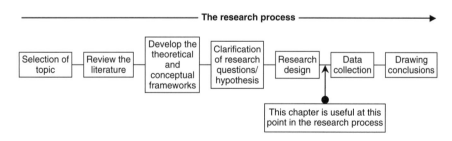

Figure 8.1 The research process: making ethics applications

Introduction

The overall ethical consideration of a research project is vital because it helps ensure you behave properly as a researcher. Your project must be considered in terms of beneficence, which is the act of doing something good, ensuring your project does no harm, you respect autonomy and you are just. Therefore this chapter is essential reading for everyone who is undertaking a research project. Consideration of your research and behaving ethically is important to good research practice. This chapter will also help with the practicality of applying for ethical approval from your awarding institution, if required, and creating an informed consent form.

Carrying out an independent research project will bring you lots of new experiences and being independent greatly enhances your learning. Being independent in your research may also mean that this is the first time that you have had to consider your behaviour ethically as a researcher. This chapter will help you understand what ethics in research means and will provoke you to think critically about your own research project in regards to ethics and ethical behaviour. It begins by asking questions such as what ethics are, and explores some of the issues of participant rights as well as codes of conduct. It will then highlight some of the specific issues that you will have to consider, such as informed consent and data confidentiality. With this grounding in place the final third of the chapter will help guide you in making an ethics application for your own research as well as designing an informed consent form for your project.

Why consider ethics in research?

This may be the first time you have had to consider the topic of ethics in research. It is a very complex and thought-provoking subject in its own right and making an ethics application may be one of the major hurdles that you have to overcome in your research project. It helps to consider the ethics of your work from the very beginning of your project, because ethics impact upon the topic you choose, the way you recruit your participants and collect your data, and how you handle the data once you gather it. Many institutions will require an ethical application to check that these things are being considered and controlled. Seeking the ethical approval from your institution is essential to allow your research to progress.

As a researcher, you can easily get caught up in your topic and subject area. Your first consideration is often how you can find the answers to the questions you work on; unfortunately, the health, safety and well-being of those who participate in your research can be secondary. It should not be like that of course, but often the enthusiasm of carrying out a project can take away from equal consideration of your research's impact on the health, safety and well-being of your participants. This will come with experience and time. Consideration of ethics is not only a practical consideration but is also an essential consideration for good research practice.

What are research ethics?

Consideration of research ethics is important for you as a researcher and for your research project; it is important that you understand what research ethics are and how they relate to you, your participants and your research design. There can be a lot of discussion about ethical values and how these relate to moral values. They are not inseparable but we do need to make a distinction between them. We only do this because the aim of this book is not to discuss them but to look at how ethics will impact upon your research. The further reading list will offer a text that is an excellent discussion of research ethics in sport and exercise.

Morals are distinct from ethics. Morals can be thought of as a personal set of unwritten values that are unique to each person and are used as a framework to help decision making and regulate behaviour in our everyday lives. Ethics and ethical values are similar in that they are a framework to help decision making and regulate behaviour, but the difference is that ethics are contextualised and can sometimes be regulated by others, such as ethics committees, or written for organisations, as in codes of conduct. So from that we can deduce that as a person, you have your own moral values that you live by; as a researcher, you have those as well as ethical values to work by.

Ethical values and codes are important to research. As a researcher we can be very enthusiastic about our particular projects and research areas. This enthusiasm can sometimes lead us to not see clearly or understand well how we can infringe on the moral and legal rights of those who participate in our research. There are examples of research in the past that have contravened what would be considered by many to be ethical behaviour and the decisions and behaviour of the researcher has certainly damaged the participants in some way. Sometimes participants have been very seriously hurt, not only physically but psychologically or socially. Ethics are there to help protect participants and ourselves as researchers, and to also help ensure good research practice. Ethics also relate to you as a researcher to help guide you in good research practice, particularly in regard to scientific honesty and preventing the publishing of fraudulent results.

Research ethics and legal liability

Research ethics are closely linked to some laws and it is important to remember that *you* may feel that you have behaved ethically, but you cannot escape or use excuses when it comes to compliance with the law. Many of these laws have come about through events in history. The following timeline below gives an interesting overview into how some of the laws, acts and codes that are now in place have come about over time.

- Early 1900s. In the early 1900s there was little concern for or consideration of ethics in research and no formal regulations regarding the ethical use of human participants in research.
- 1930s/1940s. Nazi doctors experimented on prisoners in cold water to see how long they would survive.
- 1946 – the Nuremberg Code. On 9 December 1946, an American military tribunal opened criminal proceedings against 23 leading German physicians and administrators for their willing participation in war crimes and crimes against humanity. Among the charges were that German physicians conducted medical experiments on thousands of concentration camp prisoners without their consent. Most of the participants of these experiments died or were permanently crippled as a result. As a direct result of the trial, the Nuremberg Code was established in 1948, stating that *the voluntary consent of the human subject is absolutely essential*, making it clear that participants should give consent and that the benefits of research must outweigh the risks. Although it did not carry the force of law, the Nuremberg Code was the first international document which advocated voluntary participation and informed consent.
- 1961 – the Milgram experiments. This was a series of social psychology experiments conducted by Yale University psychologist Stanley Milgram, which measured the willingness of study participants to obey an authority figure who instructed them to perform acts that conflicted with their personal conscience. This experiment could be seen to raise some ethical issues as Stanley Milgram deceived his participants, and put them under more pressure than many believe was necessary.

- 1964 – Declaration of Helsinki. In 1964, the World Medical Association established recommendations guiding medical doctors in biomedical research involving human subjects. The Declaration governs international research ethics and defines rules for *research combined with clinical care* and *non-therapeutic research*. The Declaration of Helsinki was revised in 1975, 1983, 1989 and 1996 and is the basis for Good Clinical Practices used today.

Issues addressed in the Declaration of Helsinki include:

  o Research protocols should be reviewed by an independent committee prior to initiation.
  o Informed consent from research participants is necessary.
  o Research should be conducted by medically/scientifically qualified individuals.
  o Risks should not exceed benefits.

- 1966. Dr Henry Beecher produced *Ethics and Clinical Medicine* which is an analysis of questionable medical research. This highlighted many issues that required consideration.
- 1966. The first Research Ethics Committee (REC) was established in the UK.
- 1971 – The Stanford prison experiment. The Stanford prison experiment was a study of the psychological effects of becoming a prisoner or prison guard. The experiment was conducted in 1971 by a team of researchers led by Psychology Professor Philip Zimbardo at Stanford University. The experiment was widely criticised as being unethical and unscientific. Current ethical standards of psychology would not permit such a study to be conducted today.
- 2001. European Union Directive 2001/20/EC. This European Directive relates to the implementation of good clinical practice in the conduct of clinical trials on medicinal products for human use.

There are also other legal elements related to but not directly referring to research ethics that have been introduced through the years, such as the Data Protection Act. Legislation brings a number of rights, and participant rights are highlighted below.

Participant rights

The participants for your research project are human subjects, and they have universal human rights that must be adhered to. In ensuring your research project is ethical you must give consideration as to how you can protect and enshrine the human rights of those who participate. Put simply, you must take care at all times that your participants are protected from physical, mental and social harm and that you respect their rights. Most participants would be considered autonomous, that is, able to make their own choices, given the right information, however, it is worthwhile highlighting that it is possible that your research project may wish to use as participants those who would be considered to have diminished autonomy. These participants would be considered vulnerable and vulnerable participants could be children or adults who may have learning or communication difficulties, for example. Vulnerable participants can still be considered for your research project but you will have to have greater consideration to be able to ensure they and you are protected, for example by carrying out a Criminal Records Bureau check.

Codes of conduct

Codes of conduct are a tool that professional organisations use to help guide their members to abide by principles that will maintain their organisation's professional reputation. They will often include aspects of ethical behaviour. Sport and exercise science governing bodies have codes of conduct, and these are very useful starting points when considering ethics within your research project.

With the range of professional organisations to which a researcher in sport can belong there may be occasions when the codes of conduct do not agree. An example of this is an inconsistency in the number of blood samples that may be taken from a child. One organisation may recommend a certain number of samples, another may recommend less. You may be a member of both organisations and have a study that takes a number of samples that would be considered within one organisation's code of conduct but not that of the other. Inconsistencies such as this require personal consideration and the making of a personal ethical decision that should be justifiable, before then submitting it to outside scrutiny.

Research approaches also can cause differences between codes of conduct. Sport and exercise science research tends to be positivistic, and draws heavily upon medical research traditions in ethical behaviour, particularly the idea of informed consent. The growth of sociological research in exercise, health and sport has meant that much work has been done deceptively, as a participant observer. This contravenes this prime medical tenet of informed consent, and again a personal ethical choice is needed that should be justifiable before allowing outside scrutiny. So whilst codes of conduct are very worthwhile, it still comes down to maintaining your own personal ethical values and having confidence that you are within those values.

Informed consent

The gaining of informed consent from your participant is one of the methods that are employed to help ensure your participant does not suffer and you do no harm in your research project. It is a safeguard and an important one. Understanding the idea of informed consent requires examination of the two components of this concept: your participants being informed, and them giving consent.

We are autonomous beings, that is, we are capable of making independent choices. To be able to make a choice properly, that is, an informed choice, we need to know some things about the choices we have. If we ask someone to participate in a research project, we must respect their choice to participate or not to participate. They should not feel any pressure or be coerced in any way. There can be no exceptions to this ideal. With vulnerable populations, special care is needed to ensure the consent gained is ethical, and will often require full understanding from those who act on their behalf. When giving information, it must be easily understood. It is vital to provide information in a way that is understandable to your participants. That information should detail what will happen in terms of procedure and what might happen in terms of both potential benefits to them and potential risks in their participation. This information should include all possibilities and both the negatives and positives. If you do achieve this then it will satisfy the *informed* part of the informed consent process.

Giving consent is the second part to this process. Giving consent can only happen if the person giving it is able to make a rational, mature and considered judgement of the information you have provided. It is equally important that the consent they give is free from coercion, influence, and threat of sanction, and is voluntary. They can of course withdraw consent at anytime. How to write an informed consent form for your research project is explained later in the chapter.

Data and confidentiality

Every participant has a right to the data you keep about them to be kept private and confidential. This is another responsibility that you, as the researcher, have to carry and it is a serious one. There are two main areas that need consideration when keeping data confidential: how you store it, and in what form you publish it.

It is likely you will gather some very personal information about your participants: details such as their name, address, contact numbers, dates of birth and a lot more. You will also gather some sensitive data. Consider the idea of collecting fitness data about an athlete and what that may be worth in competitive terms to opponents. It may seem normal to you as a researcher to hold that information, but that information in the wrong hands can cause a lot of problems, such as identity theft. Therefore, it must be kept securely. If you keep it electronically then you can secure it with a password, either on the computer, or on the file itself. If you have it paper-based, then it should be stored somewhere where only you have access, such as in a locked filing cabinet. Your supervisor may be willing to let you use space in their secure storage cabinets or office. Remember that you are liable for that data and its safe storage so be very careful with it.

The second part to handling sensitive data and participant confidentiality is keeping any published material anonymous. When data is grouped, it is relatively straightforward to keep individuals' data anonymous. You may just list participants as numbers or letters. If it is a case study then you may want to use a false name. Do not be too inventive here. Jane or John Doe would be fine. The abiding rule is a participant's data should never be identifiable from its published form.

Ethics applications

You should now have a better understanding of some of the potential ethical pitfalls that could arise in your research project. It was important to get a brief overview of ethics so that any practical application is fully understood as to why you are doing what you do. This next section will give you advice on some of the things you need to consider when making an ethics application for you research project. Your institution and supervisor will be able to provide more detail and guidance on exactly what the format of the application should be and to whom it should be submitted and the process that follows that submission.

Understanding who the application will go to can help a lot when writing it. Most institutions will have an ethics committee who will scrutinise the ethical application and will either approve it, ask for some changes or reject it. Ethics committees normally comprise a range of people from a range of backgrounds. These will include some academic members, some professionals and some lay people. There are two things to remember about these committees.

- Ethics committees do not consider the academic merit of work. So, when writing your ethics application you are not trying to gain good marks or show your depth of knowledge, unless it has been designed to be part of the assessment process, so the style of writing the application will be very different to the way you would write reports or essays. Essentially you are writing for a committee to read, not to impress.

- Ethics committees normally have some non-academic members or lay people. They, and possibly even academic members, will not necessarily understand the technicalities of your intended research project. So try to write very clearly and concisely in language that is easily understood by people who have no specific background knowledge in the area of your research. If you do not do this, the application is likely to be rejected. If they cannot understand the application, they cannot consider its ethics.

Before you consider making the ethics application you must be confident and sure about the project design, the type of participants you want, the methods you intend to use and how you will deal with the data. This is because the ethics approval process will need to assess these aspects and if they change after the committee has examined your application, this can affect the status of the ethics approval. The committee are also likely to only sit at certain dates. This means you will need to plan when the application needs to be submitted, build in some safety time if there is a problem and remember you cannot normally start the project until the ethics have been approved.

The application

Each institution will have a specific procedure and format for ethics applications; be sure to consult your supervisor or seek guidance from your institution on how to make an application. Typically an ethics application will want information on the following headings.

Project design

A brief understanding of the research projects aims, how it is designed, methods of data collection and consideration of data analysis will help the committee understand the project and also allow them to begin to judge if the research is worthwhile and valuable resources are not being wasted. It also allows an assessment of where there is possible risk of harm. For example your protocol may require dehydrated participants; how you will achieve and monitor this as well as ensure their health and safety would be something the committee will want to know.

Relationship with participants

This is a very important area to consider in making an ethics application. This is because the participants are the ones that are most likely exposed to harm. Consideration is given to how many and the type of participants that will be recruited as well as the recruitment and selection methods used. One issue that can cause concern is the paying of participants to take part in your project. The paying of participants can be considered an incentive for them to take part in a study from which they would normally withdraw. Payment like this is different to reimbursement of expenses, as sometimes you would not want to inconvenience subjects financially while they take part in your study. How this is administered needs to be made very clear.

Confidentiality and data protection

Whenever you make observations of participants the data gathered should be treated as confidentially as possible. Generally that means only you as a researcher, and potentially your supervisor, has access to or knows of the identities of the participants.

Using codes or assigning numbers to participants and their research record helps protect anonymity. Also data is normally presented back as a group of participants rather than individuals. This grouping of data also helps mask identity.

In the UK, the Data Protection Act requires anyone who handles personal information to comply with a number of important principles. It also gives individuals rights over their personal information; these requirements should be studied carefully to ensure you comply.

Relationships with commissioners of the work

Information on any relationship with commissioners of the work helps to ensure that any potential conflict of interest is negated. It is not common for issues like this to be dealt with in a first research project, but it is possible. Normally your supervisor will be able to ensure this aspect of ethics is clear.

> ### Learning Activity 8.1
>
> From this you may now be able to draft a research ethics application. Your institution is likely to have a standard format or a guide to completing one. You may also be able to view examples of completed and approved previous applications.

Creating an informed consent form

The ethics committee will want to see the information sheet that is presented to possible participants of your research project. They will want to see that the requirements of informed consent are being met. You will also need to create an informed consent form for the participants in your project, and this next section details how to create one.

There is a lot of variation in terms of content, language and length of informed consent forms. Your institution and supervisor will advise you on this, but take care to avoid generic templates that you may see in some texts and available through the internet. Remember your project is very specific and likely to be unique and because of that the information related to your project in terms of benefits and risks is likely to be very specific and unique. Simply using a generic informed consent form will not normally satisfy the requirements of gaining informed consent from your participants.

As a guide the following components should be in an informed consent form:

- background and invitation to participate;
- explanation of procedures;
- potential risks and discomforts;
- potential benefits;

- rights of inquiry and withdrawal;
- signatures of participant and witness.

Background and invitation to participate

Always consider the informed consent form from the participants' point of view, because it is essentially for them, so in this section provide them with some clear and easily understood information about the background to the study, why it is worth doing and why you are asking them to participate in it.

Explanation of procedures

Sufficient information needs to be provided here about what will happen to the participant. Consider the necessary detail of the procedures, pre- and post-test assessments, interventions or treatments and how much time they will be required to give up to participate. You must not gloss over or deliberately omit something; it would be unethical to suddenly announce to your participant something you had *forgotten* to include or explain fully, such as a muscle biopsy!

Potential risks and discomforts

Describing the potential risks and discomforts a participant may be *reasonably* expected to encounter in participating in your research study allows them to make an informed choice as to whether to participate or not, so consider risks that may be:

- physical;
- psychological;
- social;
- legal or economic.

You may also describe here what steps are in place to negate those risks, such as having a qualified first aider present, for example in case of physical harm.

Potential benefits

Where there is risk, there is normally some benefit too. Potential benefits that could be accrued from participating in the study can be considered in two ways: benefits to them personally, such as getting fitter, and benefits to society as a whole. Do not over-exaggerate potential benefits but if there are clearly some, state them. There may not be any potential benefit to the participant, but often the study and its advancement of knowledge to society as a whole is an important consideration and one that should not be ignored.

Rights of inquiry and withdrawal

It is important, particularly when some participants may be overawed by a laboratory and white coat setting, that they should feel free to ask questions, and expect answers. This is particularly important when seeking their informed consent, but stays true over the whole of the research project. Good practice would also be to allow the contact details of those supervising the project to be available should the participant want to seek higher authority.

They also have a right to withdraw from the study at any time. As a researcher this can be frustrating but it is very important that that right is enshrined and no coercion or pressure should be brought to bear otherwise. Of course, good practice would be to recruit more participants than you need because some withdrawal is always likely.

Another ethical issue to consider is ensuring that by consenting there is no withdrawal or waiver of any legal rights or privileges. This is also true for the researcher; the act of gaining consent does not absolve you from your responsibilities or liability.

Signatures of subject and witness

Although informed consent can be given verbally, good practice would be to ensure a signed copy that is suitably witnessed is recorded and kept safe. Many informed consent forms have a short statement reinforcing the participant's right to withdraw; before getting them to sign it, ensure you check that all the questions or queries have been answered or satisfied.

Learning Activity 8.2

From this you may now be able to draft an informed consent form. Your institution is likely to have a standard format or a guide to completing one. You may also be able to view examples of previous forms.

You as a researcher

One final consideration while we discuss ethics is you as a researcher. This chapter has concentrated on protection of the participants in your research project, but it is equally important that you are aware of and take care to avoid putting yourself as a researcher in a position of potential harm. Carrying out a research project could expose you to potential risks such as:

- actual or threatened violence, psychological harm, unwanted sexual advances, etc.;
- injury travelling to or from field research;
- allegations that you as a researcher have acted inappropriately;
- implication in illegal activities.

Consider at all times your own personal security. Good practice would be to carry out a risk assessment for your project. When you carry out a risk assessment, also consider in that assessment the risks to you. If you have any concerns discuss these with your supervisor or someone in your institution.

Chapter Review

The take-home messages from this chapter are:

- An understanding of ethics will really help make sense of why an ethics application for your research project should be completed. Ethics in research is a very complex and thought-provoking area and this chapter does not do justice to the issues that can present themselves. For those who enjoy thinking through the philosophy of something, ethics can be a great subject to explore.
- There has been guidance on how to complete an ethics application and an informed consent form presented in this chapter. Each research project is unique and therefore every application and informed consent completed for that project is unique. This is general guidance only. Consult the guidance from your institution to be thorough.

Further Reading

Ethics is a topic that really requires a lot of further reading to understand properly. I would suggest, from a practical point of view, that it is essential to read the codes of conduct that organisations such as the British Association of Sport and Exercise Sciences (BASES) or the American College of Sports Medicine (ACSM) provide on their websites. Codes of conduct also exist for the regulatory bodies in particular countries for disciplines such as nutrition and psychology.

One author who has produced an excellent text that really discusses the issues in the ethics of sport and exercise is Mike McNamee, and I would highly recommend reading it.

- McNamee, M (2006) *Research Ethics in Exercise, Health and Sports Sciences.* Abingdon: Routledge.

Or see Steve and Amanda Olivier's article 'Informed consent in sport science', *Sportscience*, 5(1); available at www.sportsci.org/jour/0101/so.htm.

Chapter 9
Writing the how

Learning Objectives

This chapter will help you to be able to:

- understand the format and structure of your research report;
- understand the conventions of scientific writing;
- consider the likely audience of your research report and adjust your writing style to suit that audience.

You will also be able to:

- write an initial draft of your method.

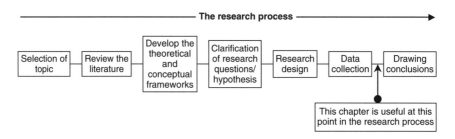

Figure 9.1   The research process: writing the how

Introduction

This chapter is essential for everyone who has to present a finished research project. Presenting your work is the culmination of your research project and to ensure that credit is given it is essential that the quality of that presentation reflects the quality of the research project itself. This chapter is the second of four chapters that break up the writing of your research project into manageable sections. By the end of each chapter you will be able to write first drafts of the sections covered by that chapter.

- *Writing the why* covered the introduction and literature review.
- *Writing the how* covers the method.

- *Writing what you have found* will cover the results.
- *Writing the so what* will cover the discussion and conclusion.

If you are presenting your research project in a different format to a conventional written report, such as a poster, there are still some important aspects that are common to scientific presentation, so it is still essential reading.

Science demands reproducibility. It is not sufficient to design and carry out a research project. Others must be able to verify your findings, so your project must be reproducible, to the extent that other researchers can follow the same procedure and obtain the same or similar results. The method section is the key section to making your research reproducible.

This chapter begins by helping you to plan and consider the conventions of writing the method. It then takes each sub-heading of the method and discusses what should be included and how that section should be written. At the end there is a writing-up checklist that will help to keep your drafting of each section on track.

Planning to write the method

The method section of your research report should be structured as follows:

- title page;
- abstract;
- introduction;
- literature review;
- methods;
- results;
- discussion and conclusions;
- references;
- appendices.

In Chapter 7 I discussed how your research report should tell a story. The method section is about explaining how you did what you did in that story. It is a relatively simple section to write and can be as short or as long, as simple or as complicated as your method itself. As a guide for your writing we can use an overall structure that will logically explain to the reader what was done to collect your data. To write it to make it count, we must consider the content, including the rationale for your actions, the conventions used in the method, terminology and the style specific to the method. The method section of a research report would normally have the following sub-headings:

- participants;
- study design;
- protocol;
- apparatus;
- data analysis.

These sub-headings will be the structure to the methods section of your research report. It may be that your particular institution has different requirements, require that these be presented in a different order or combine some of the sub-headings. Check that you are meeting your institution's requirements. Later in this chapter I will expand what needs to be included under each of the sub-headings.

Now that you have an understanding of the framework within which you will be writing, you need to understand what the content of the method should be. Sometimes the hardest thing about writing this section is not what you should write, but what you should *not* write. I often see the results of the data collection in the method, perhaps because they are measured and recorded during the course of the research project, but such information should be reserved for the results section. When writing the method section, you can write that you recorded the results, or how you recorded the results, but you should not write what the results were, not yet. In the method section you are stating exactly how you went about collecting your data. You are writing what you did. You are writing the relevant and necessary elements to allow your work to be reproducible. Because this is also likely to be assessed by your academic institution, you need to add more to the method. You need to add why you did what you did; this is known as the rationale.

It is likely that the report you have to write is substantial and assessed as an academic piece of work. Because of this it is important to include the rationale for your actions in the method. Be sure that as you are relating your actions during the data collection you explain your rationale for the protocol you developed. If you allowed a two-week wash-out period between trials, why did you do that? Professional researchers will provide their rationale as a way to explain their thinking to potential critics. Of course, that is your motivation for talking about your rationale too, you are writing to make it count. In more practical terms you are also writing to your supervisor or lecturer who is evaluating your project, to make clear to them how well you comprehend the principles of the research process; explaining the rationale indicates that you understand the reasons for conducting the data collection in that way. Critical thinking is crucial.

Reflection Point

Richard told me the following when we discussed the method for his research project.

I was constantly trying to explain what I was doing to anyone who would listen but I did not really always understand why I was doing it that way. Writing a draft of my method section for the report made me start to think critically about the methods I was using. It really helped me write things because the more I had to justify my actions the more they became clearer to me.

The message that we can take from what Richard was saying is that by writing a draft method out you can start to think critically about why you are doing things a certain way. It will certainly help prepare you for awkward questions from your supervisor or lecturer.

Now we must consider the following aspects of writing the method:

- the conventions used;
- the use of terminology in the method;
- the style the method should be written in.

Convention

The normal convention of writing in the third person that was described in Chapter 7 should be followed as well in this section. It is likely to be difficult to do this as it would feel very natural to write the method section in the first person. After all you did do the work. The use of the third person helps to make sure the research report is presented in an objective format. It should also be in the past tense as the work has already been carried out. This may differ from the tense you used in writing the method in a research proposal if you wrote one; remember that a proposal would be something *you were going to do* but the method in your report is what *you have done*.

To demonstrate this here is an example of writing in the third person.

- Incorrect: *We administered a 30% carbohydrate solution.* The subject, *we*, performs the action, administered.
- Correct: *A 30% carbohydrate solution was administered.* The subject, *solution*, does not do the administering. It is acted upon, not acting.

Writing in the third person may be difficult at first but you will soon find little tricks to help word the actions you did into a third person form.

Terminology

Writing the method is one area where the use of terminology can be very prominent. It is important to use the correct terminology and to be consistent with its use. Readers of your report will scrutinise the method you have used, and will want to thoroughly understand how you collected your data and what you then did with it. Correct terminology can clarify this for the reader. Incorrect terminology will either confuse or even worse mislead the reader as to what your actions were. Inevitably there will be a need to use a certain amount of terminology and you should not be afraid to use it appropriately. Do not try to be too clever in your use of it, though. Do not use a less understood word just to demonstrate you know it, if a more commonly understood term can be used. A research report should be clear and concise and easily understood. As was highlighted in Chapter 4 some terminology can differ depending on the country. An example of this is the terminology for the hormone adrenaline. In the UK it is called adrenaline, in the USA it is often referred to as epinephrine. Consider the audience your report is likely to be read by; if you were writing it as a report for a journal based in a different country you might consider using another language dictionary. The guidelines for a particular journal will normally indicate the appropriate language and spellings.

Style

The style of writing the method section is often determined by the nature of the research project itself. Generally two approaches are taken.

- Use of sub-headings to make different sections clear.
- A narrative structure to your actions.

Where your research project is complex or uses a procedure that is complex and not well known to your readers, using sub-headings can break down complex procedures into manageable chunks. Sub-headings can offer the reader a chance to absorb each particular part. It does have the disadvantage though of sometimes lacking a cohesive narrative thread.

A narrative structure is about telling a story. In this case it is the story of the method used to collect the data. It describes what was done in the order it was done. We are used to reading about events chronologically, and so your readers will generally understand what you did if you present that information in the same way. Using a combination of a narrative structure and sub-headings can be very effective.

Be careful to avoid taking a 'recipe' approach to writing the method. You should be reporting what *did* happen, not telling the reader how to perform the method. Whilst your method should be clear enough to be reproducible, that is not to say it will be reproduced, and so does not need to be written as a recipe.

With both a sub-heading and a narrative approach remember that you are describing what happened, so you should use the past tense to refer to everything you did during the method. You are writing about something that happened at a particular time in the past, and which has already ended by the time you start writing, so simple past tense will be an appropriate tense in this section.

The next part of this chapter will help identify what should be included under each sub-heading.

Participants

This section is sometimes referred to as *subjects*; I have chosen to use the term participants throughout this text, and it refers to those who participate in your research project. Either terminology is fine, but your institution may have a preference. Within this section of the method your aim should be to:

- describe how many participants were used. This may include how many started and how many actually finished the study.
- describe how you recruited and chose your participants. Essentially, you describe your sample method.
- describe the variable characteristics, relevant to your project, of the participants. For example, age and gender may be relevant across many types of project. For physiologically based projects, variables may include height, weight and a measure of fitness, such as leg strength. Dependent on the circumstances of your research project you will decide on what is a relevant variable characteristic in your participants.

Consideration of human participants

Chapter 8 discussed ethics: how the consideration of human participants in research is vital and what protective measures are in place. In writing the method you should make reference to the protective measures you have followed to ensure that ethical consideration of the participants in your research project has been established.

Study design

This section of the method provides an overview of the formal design of the study for the reader of the report – essentially, what the independent and dependent variables are, if an experimental design has been used, or if non-experimental research has been followed, what particular method has been used to collect the data. (Chapter 3 helped identify independent and dependent variables and Chapters 5 and 6 examined experimental and non-experimental research.) The reader will want to know which designs were used, as some are more efficient or valid than others for particular types of research questions. Do not be afraid to justify why a different, and possibly more efficient or valid, method has not been used. Provide the rationale for your actions.

Protocol

This is sometimes referred to as the procedure and is the actual detail of how you carried out the data collection. I advise students who struggle with writing this part to think of what the participant went through from the moment they walked through the door to the moment they finish, and start by writing that. This approach is particularly good if your research project has used an experimental design. Many projects will not have used an experimental approach, so you will need to consider how this should be presented. A very useful tool in helping your reader to understand the procedures you have followed is to include a schematic diagram of how you have collected your data.

Consider that this section should describe the fine detail of your method of data collection. Look for the answers to the questions you might ask a peer doing a similar study, such as what order were things done in, how long was the time between trials, how were the trial orders randomised? Often the most crucial detail is measurement. You should always quantify anything you can, such as time elapsed, temperature, dose, etc.

You should also describe the controls you have in place. Many research projects, particularly those that use an experimental design, will include controls. Two things are especially important in writing about the controls you have included. Identify the control as a control, and explain what you are controlling for. An example you often see in physiological studies is that the participant completes all trials at the same time of day. This is to control for the effects of circadian rhythms. The control is the carrying out of data collection at the same time of day, to minimise the effect of circadian rhythms.

The key point to remember when writing this part is to provide the detail required for the data collection to be replicated, if they are relevant to the outcomes of the research report.

Apparatus

This is a straightforward part of the method to write. It can sometimes be called *equipment*, but that is not a suitable heading for all studies. As with the protocol you need to consider providing enough detail for the data collection to be replicated. One of the important factors to consider in this section is, *how much detail?* Be precise in providing details, but stay relevant. Ask yourself, *would it make any difference if someone replicating this research were to use apparatus that was different?* If not, you probably do not need to get too specific. If so, you should give as many details as necessary to ensure someone replicating the experiment does exactly the same as you did.

If you are describing equipment, do not be too pedantic. Items such as stop watches or pencils can be assumed to be used, but more technical items do need to be described. You may need to include model numbers and manufacturers' names.

Some research projects may use established questionnaires or inventories to gather data. It is vital that the rationale for the use of this particular questionnaire or inventory is used. It would also be important to provide full reference for it. If you have created your own measurement tool, an example of it should be included in the appendices, but do not include it in this section.

Data analysis

The method that you use to analyse your data is as important as any other part of the method. It is often a neglected part of many first-time research reports because many first-time researchers do not consider it part of the method. It is. How you analyse your data can have a massive effect on the results and hence how you interpret your findings.

As with the other sections of the method, the important consideration is to provide enough detail for your research project to be replicated by another. Include only relevant information. You do not need to tell the reader how data was described in figures and tables, or by use of descriptive statistics. What is more important is to state what descriptive and inferential tests were used, including the detail of any particular computer package that was used and the justifications for it.

Writing-up checklist

- Have you set yourself deadlines and kept to them?
- Do you write regularly?
- When you have completed your reading for one section of the method do you write it up?
- Do you check that you have covered all essential requirements of the section of the report you are working on?
- Are you taking care to stay within the required word limit and your targeted limit for that section?
- Ensure that you keep the structure of your report simple and easy to follow; use sub-headings to help structure individual sections.
- Think carefully about how you will ensure that the core chapters – i.e. *Literature review, Research methodology, Results* and *Analysis and discussion* – link together. The use of sub-headings that relate to each other may help you to avoid the trap of losing the focus of your research.
- Number tables and figures and provide titles.
- Check your referencing system is correct. Make sure you have acknowledged your sources.
- Check your bibliography for errors.

- Give yourself time to revise your writing and ask someone to proofread it for mistakes in grammar, paragraph structure, spelling and understanding.
- Avoid using jargon and technical language as much as possible. Where this is used, explain its meaning to the reader.
- Check that you have stated the aims of the research clearly.
- Remember to see your supervisor regularly for help and guidance.
- *Do not* give up – most people find it difficult to write, even those who write for a living.

We will use this checklist again later in the book and so, for ease of reference, it is also given in the Appendix to this book.

Chapter Review

The take-home messages from this chapter are:

- The method should provide enough detail for the research project to be reproducible by others, but not to provide a recipe for them to follow.
- Often the best approach to writing a method is to consider using a narrative structure with suitable sub-headings that break the information up.
- Do not include any results in this section. How that section is written will be covered in Chapter 11.

Further Reading

In previous chapters I have highlighted many key texts that are specific to sport and exercise and that I consider excellent relevant help to that particular chapter. Most of those texts will have useful guidance on how to write an introduction or literature review. In addition, there are a number of books that provide excellent help for writing in general. For a list of these titles, please see the 'Further Reading' section at the end of Chapter 7.

Chapter 10
Data analysis

This chapter will help you to be able to:

- understand how to organise and process quantitative data;
- carry out descriptive and inferential statistical procedures;
- organise and process qualitative data.

You will also be able to:

- carry out an initial exploration and analysis of your data.

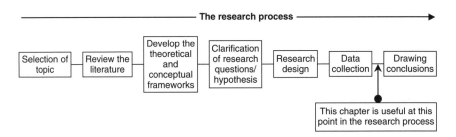

Figure 10.1 The research process: data analysis

Introduction

If you have got as far as collecting data for your research project, then this chapter is for you. It is from the data collected that you will draw your conclusions, so to understand the basic processes in data analysis is vital. This chapter is not designed to show you how to do the specific tests, but rather it outlines how to carry out that analysis generally. It provides an overview and guidance on how to begin the processes. The further reading at the end of this chapter will give you a guide as to an appropriate text to read for your project to gain a deeper understanding of the analysis of your data.

The aim of any research project is to logically and systematically investigate a topic and then report the findings. In the same way that you approached the method in collecting your data, the way you now deal with that data is logical and systematic.

To simply report the mass of data that you will have collected without any processing of it would be overwhelming for all but the most dedicated followers of your topic area and so there needs to be a method in which data can be organised and presented, so the key findings can be presented in a clear and objective way. As with the project so far, there is a process you can follow to help you achieve this.

This chapter begins by discussing the need for you to understand the nature of the data you have collected. It then examines how to use descriptive statistics to help start to make sense of what you have and then to be able to describe it for others. Using descriptive statistics is also a first step for those who are testing a hypothesis. The descriptive statistics then lead on to the inferential statistics to provide evidence to support or reject the hypothesis. Both of the sections will briefly suggest ways the findings from your statistical procedures can be presented, although this is covered in more detail in Chapter 11, *Writing what you have found*. Some common problems in data analysis are also discussed.

If your data is qualitative, then neither descriptive nor inferential statistics may be appropriate. There are a number of methods to analyse qualitative data, and the final section of this chapter will give you an overview of how to deal with this kind of data.

A note of caution: this chapter is not designed to give a thorough understanding of statistics and statistical procedures – there are plenty of good texts and websites that will do that and some of these will be highlighted in the further reading section of this chapter – rather, it is designed to help you understand what the general methods are and how they will help you in completing and presenting your research project.

Understanding and preparing your data

Throughout your research project, when you have written drafts of your literature review and methodology, you will have collected and organised a large amount of material. You have developed skills in organising, sorting and presenting this material. Those skills have helped you understand and prepare the information you have. Now you have large amounts of different material, the data you have collected, and it is time to organise, sort and present this. This is called data analysis and one of the tools that makes this task a lot easier and ready for presentation to your readers is statistics.

I know that many a groan is heard whenever the word statistics is uttered, but try not to fall into the same trap as so many others. Statistics are simply tools that help you do a job. The skill is picking the right tool for the job and learning how to use that tool correctly. You have already done this, by learning to use a measuring tool in your method or to write a literature review, so embrace statistics in the same way.

An important point to remember is that you are a sport and exercise researcher, not a statistician. Statisticians are experts in a completely different subject area. The language of mathematics and logic run through them, in the same way the language of research and your sport and exercise topic now runs through you. Research is a team activity and seeking the advice, help and guidance of someone with a greater statistical knowledge than you is a desirable thing.

What is important to understand is that you need enough statistical knowledge to enable you to describe your data and test it for its significance. Statistics are simply tools that help you understand the findings in an organised way and we can split statistics into two areas: descriptive statistics and inferential statistics.

Having an understanding of and then preparing your data for analysis is essential to producing quality outcomes for your research project. A common problem, which I shall expand more upon later in the chapter, is a failure to organise and explore the data prior to analysis. It is very useful to start this process as soon as you can. You do not have to wait until all the data is collected; you can start to explore and organise your data right from the moment the first bit is collected. This should continue until all of it is collected and you are ready to do a final analysis. This will make the whole process of data analysis much easier.

Before we go any further you should identify whether your data is quantitative or qualitative. If it is quantitative then read on; if it is qualitative you may consider skipping these initial sections and going to the section on qualitative data analysis.

Consideration of data analysis should be made at the planning stage and you should at least know the type of data you are likely to have. Is it nominal, ordinal, interval or ratio? Interval or ratio data are the data types normally derived from direct measurement of some sort, as you would find in a physiological or biomechanical research project. These types of data can often be subjected to both descriptive and inferential statistical techniques.

Nominal or ordinal data is the type of data you are likely to collect through surveys and questionnaires. If your data is nominal or ordinal, then the descriptive statistics are important, as these are the methods likely to be used in analysing your data. These are generalisations, however, and your research methods lecturers will be able to guide you more. Understanding what type of data you have is a big step towards being able to choose the right tools to analyse it.

Understanding your data is not just about being aware of the type of data but also the nature of the information. It is about starting to see the hard results of the method you have carried out. By looking over the data, you start to see patterns. They may or may not be the patterns you expected. Values may be higher or lower than you predicted. I often think as I collect data in research projects I have done how often the actual data does not always reflect what I thought I saw when I was collecting it. The numbers appear to tell a different story to my observations. This can be surprising and thought provoking. It may be that simply observing is biased in some way. The numbers are the hard objective factual result of the method though, and that is one of the reasons why it is worth exploring them and getting to know your data right from the very first collection, because it is what you will rely on to draw objective conclusions for your research project. To understand the nature of your data better, organising it first is a useful initial step.

Organising your data can be difficult. Often you will not really appreciate how much data you will collect or in what form it will be until you start to collect it. Many measurement tools will provide a lot of information. You may have to dissect the bits you want from the whole mass of it that you get. This is one reason why some practice runs of data collection are essential. Having a peer be a participant for you and trial running them through the data collection method is not only good practice for you and the method itself but will also give you ideas on how to organise and deal with the data you will get.

So when thinking about how to prepare your data you have to think and plan ahead. A good idea is to link how you have recorded your data in the method of collection to how you are going to analyse it. It is likely some sort of computer spreadsheet will be used in the analyses you wish to do, so why not make the way you collect and then transfer the data match the format of the spreadsheet? This can have advantages. It will save time and there is less confusion about how data is transferred from one place to another. This often leads to fewer errors. It can be disadvantageous too. In particular, you tend to get less of a feel for the data because you transfer it over so smoothly.

Learning Activity 10.1

Develop a spreadsheet that you can use as a data recording sheet; it should offer a simple way to record, view and then analyse your data, all in line with the computer package you intend to use for your analyses. This will take a little practice and refinement to get right, so some preparatory work is needed. It will save so much time in the long run though and cut down errors, as the less moving or rearranging of data you can do the better.

This linking of data recording sheets to your method of data analysis also allows preliminary work with the data as soon as you have it. Once you have data from one participant, you have the data to work with. The next section covering descriptive statistics will cover how to work with this data in more detail. You should aim to do some preliminary analyses as your data starts to come together.

One of the problems you will encounter in preparing your data are missing values. You may have missed recording a measurement, or something stopped you recording it at the time. Missing data values are a fact of life in research projects and so luckily many methods of analysis can cope with a missing value or two. If you have too much missing data it may be impossible to analyse and a rethink of what you are doing may be needed. What is important is that you do not corrupt the data. Do not add the values you think they may have been, or correct values because they look wrong. Instead examine the numbers you have, using descriptive statistics, and then decide if the missing values would really change those descriptive numbers. In the case of a missing value or two it is unlikely they would. Descriptive statistics also help identify erroneous or outlying values. It is best at this early stage in data analysis that any decision you make on missing values is a sound one. The best advice is to discuss these things with your supervisor. Whatever the course of action you take, you must ensure that the data you deal with is accurate.

Reflection Point

Richard told me the following when we discussed his research project.

I was really worried about the data analysis part of the project. Numbers are not my thing and talk of statistics scared me. Your advice of getting into it early was the right thing to do. I found it manageable. The more I did, the better it felt and the way I understood things just shot up until I was actually enjoying dealing with the numbers and watching the project grow with each new set.

The message is clear here. Data analysis cannot be avoided in a research project and if anything it should be embraced. By beginning to approach the processes you have to follow early it can be made a lot easier than you think it will be.

Descriptive statistics

As the name suggests descriptive statistics are statistical methods that describe the characteristics of a data set. They are the transformation of raw data from an organised form into a *reader-friendly* form. This transformation is important. Consider the mass of data you have collected. No one, including you, can make any real sense of what you have and until you can you cannot draw any conclusions from it. Transforming data into a reader-friendly form is about describing that data in a clear concise way.

For some research projects it may be enough to use descriptive statistics only to offer analysis of the data. The research may have been intended to be purely descriptive. For other research projects descriptive statistics are the first step in the data analysis, followed by inferential statistics.

So, how to use descriptive statistics in your research project? Remember you are describing the data to allow you to either begin or allow further analysis and to present it to a reader of your work. Normally the information you present in descriptive statistical analysis is related to the measures of central tendency of the data, and the degree of spread or variation of that data about its centrality.

Measures of central tendency	Measures of dispersion	Measures of variation
Average (or mean) Median Mode	Range	Standard deviation

Table 10.1: Methods of describing central tendency, spread and variation

From your research methods lecturers you should have a full understanding of what each of these represent and how to calculate these values. In my research methods class, to help illustrate these concepts, I do the following activity. I ask everyone in the class to stand up and come out. For this exercise I ask each person their height in centimetres. This gives a numerical value I can work with. Each person then represents a single data point that has been measured. At the front of the class I then ask them all to organise themselves into height order, shortest to tallest. In the same way, doing this with a set of data points from your data will give the spread of data. Simply take the shortest height from the tallest, or the smallest value from the greatest value. To determine a measure of centrality, such as the median, I simply identify the middle person. This person is also likely to be close to the mean, as long as I do not have anyone too tall or small who may throw that value out and I have enough people to measure. Variation is also easy to see, as it is the difference between each individual. Of course this exercise is just to illustrate the concepts, using their heights as data points. I then do the actual calculations of course, but more often than not it works out and I can always explain why, if not. With a single data set you can do the same type of exercise and with the findings you will be able to describe the central point of the data, its spread and its variation.

Gain an understanding of each descriptive statistical tool, what it is good and not so good at describing, and what affects it. Then you can choose the one most appropriate to your data to report.

Reporting descriptive statistics

Using the descriptive statistics as tools to start to logically and systematically analyse your data is the first stage of the process of analysis. You are also likely to present these findings in some way in your research report and so you should consider what and how to present them. Chapter 11, *Writing what you have found*, will cover how to write the results section in much more detail but here are some guidelines. How you choose to present your descriptive statistics is usually a choice between using text, tables, or graphs in some way. Your institution may have guidelines on what should be included in the results and you should seek guidance from your supervisor to ensure you are on the right track. Different journals and associations will also have guidelines on how the statistics should be presented; often institutions use a particular journal or association as a guide to how their own data analysis should be presented. Reading journal articles from different sources and examining how those articles have presented the descriptive statistics is a great start.

If you choose to present your descriptive statistics as text or in a table, normally a measure of central tendency and variation are presented together. These are usually the mean and the standard variation. This can give an experienced reader an understanding of both a measure of centrality of your data and the variation within it, or where most of your data points fall and how they spread. When numbers are presented in a table they are usually presented to two decimal places.

Another method of reporting descriptive statistics is by using graphs. Graphs are very useful when you have a lot of means to present, as the information can be viewed easily. Different graphs are more suitable to different types of data. For example a bar graph would be good to present means of different groups; a line graph is a good method of presenting means over time. Other types of graph, such as a pie chart, are good ways of showing different categories. Normally you would not duplicate how you present your data. You would not normally include both a table and a graph of the same findings. However you present the material, always remember that it is about communication, communicating in as clear and concise a way as possible. Ask yourself whether the way you are presenting your information is clear and concise. For some research projects, data analysis and presenting the results of that analysis through descriptive statistics will be enough. Other projects will use inferential statistics to further analyse the data, and here descriptive statistics play a role too.

Inferential statistics

With descriptive statistics you can describe your data, or describe the characteristics of your participants. Inferential statistics go one step further and allow you to determine whether a relationship or difference exists to a statistically significant level in your data. To draw an inference from something is to draw a conclusion from evidence and that is really what a research project that has a hypothesis is all about: examining a problem, investigating it and bringing the results of that investigation to a conclusion by drawing an inference from the findings.

To be able to draw an inference from a data set you need a starting point that will act as a reference against which you can compare the findings. Normally the population from which the sample of participants is drawn is the reference point. When you measure something in enough people you will get a lot of data points. You are then able to draw a frequency curve from each of these data points, and normally that curve would resemble a bell shape. At this point talk of inferential statistics could start to get a little complex with statistical technicalities, but consider this: how much does the bell-shaped curve you have with the data from your participants differ in distance and shape from the bell-shaped reference curve? This will determine the degree of inference you can draw from any statistical test looking for a difference or relationship. Descriptive statistics also play a role in inferential statistics, as it is descriptive statistics that provide an easy method to describe the shape of the bell-shaped curve of your data.

Choosing an inferential statistical test

This book is not designed to cover specific statistical methods in any detail but to aid you in carrying out your research project from start to finish, so I must emphasise here that additional knowledge and understanding of the statistical treatment of data is essential. You should make real efforts to understand statistics as then not only can you make an informed decision about which statistical test to choose but you will also completely understand the result that it gives.

That said, there are some ways that a specific inferential statistical test can be chosen for your particular project, if you understand and know a little about its design and the type of data you have. Use the chart below to find your particular test considering the design and the data you have.

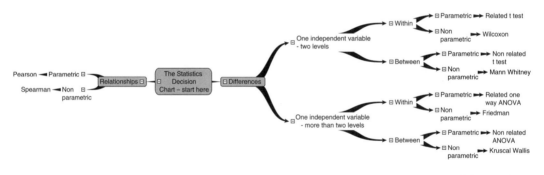

Figure 10.2 Statistical decision chart

This statistical decision chart is a useful tool to identify the particular test you need to use. Now you must actually carry out the test and interpret the results of that test to determine the significance of your results.

Interpretation of the results of an inferential statistical test

We use descriptive statistics to simply describe what is happening in our data. With inferential statistics we try to reach conclusions that extend beyond the immediate data alone. For instance, we use inferential statistics to make a judgement on the probability that an observed difference between groups is a significant one as opposed to a difference that may have occurred by chance.

Inferential statistics are useful in experimental and quasi-experimental research designs and a simple inferential test can be used when you want to compare the average performance of two groups on a single measure to see if there is a difference. For example, you might want to know whether a group of athletes differ in sprint times when they take a caffeine pill or not. An inferential statistical test will tell you this if you can interpret the results of the test correctly.

Rather than try to explain how to interpret the results from each test, which would not be feasible for this text as there are so many different tests and the interpretation of the results of each test is different, I will explain a few concepts that you need to understand.

The calculated value and critical value

An inferential statistical test is simply a formula that uses your data to produce a value. That value is known as the calculated value and on its own is just a number. You can infer nothing from it on its own. You need to compare that value to a critical value. This critical value comes from tables calculated by statisticians but now is more likely to be contained in the output of your computer's statistical package. Each test has rules as to how the calculated value should be compared against the critical value. Understanding these rules and comparing the calculated to the critical value will then allow you to interpret whether the value you have shows significance or not when compared to the alpha level. To know what the alpha value means, read about probability.

Probability

The probability of something happening can range from zero, in that it will definitely not happen, to one hundred per cent, meaning it definitely will. Despite what you may think, probabilities of zero or one hundred per cent do not really exist in research. There is always the slightest chance you have the results that you have purely by chance. In research, probability refers to the probability of your results occurring by chance rather than by your own design. Establishing a level of probability above which you accept that the results have been produced by chance rather than by design is arbitrary, but convention would normally say a probability of less than five per cent would be accepted as significant. This is known as an alpha of 0.05. In some research, it may be even less, perhaps as low as one per cent. This means there is even less possibility the results are a product of chance. Essentially, an alpha of 0.05 or 0.01 means you are setting a level above which you are willing to accept the results are because of your actions. Many statistical packages will give you a calculated and a critical value and also interpret those values and give you a probability.

If you can understand the concepts of calculated and critical values and how they can give you a probability, you are well on the way to understanding the results of an inferential statistical test. The texts highlighted in the further reading list later will give you a much greater understanding of these statistical concepts.

Reporting inferential statistics

Very surprisingly the reporting of the results of inferential statistical tests appears very simple. There is however a very specific format and style that should be followed when doing it.

The American Psychological Association (APA) produces a very detailed and specific set of guidelines on how to report the findings from inferential statistical tests, and many institutions have adopted these as their own guidelines. You should of course refer to your supervisor, but below is an example of the correct use of APA formatting.

You may notice in the example there is no discussion of critical values, null and alternative hypotheses, nor of accepting or rejecting any hypothesis. Instead, the narrative indicates to a knowledgeable reader that the null hypothesis was rejected and the alternative hypothesis was supported simply by saying that the result was statistically significant. Similarly, if the results were not significant, it is understood the null hypothesis was retained, and no support was found for the alternative hypothesis. These are clear examples of the writer considering the audience. By presenting the information in such a way, the reader who is capable and understands this will correctly interpret the result. You may feel it necessary to state such things, however, to demonstrate your understanding, and your supervisor may also want you to, but correct presentation of results can supersede this.

> *A study compared psychological scores for the motivation of footballers to those of a randomly selected class of students at the same university. Footballers (M = 79.71, SD = 11.57) expressed significantly higher levels of motivation than did the randomly selected students (M = 70.92, SD = 13.64), t(40) = 2.22, p =0.016, one-tailed, d =0.69. Alpha = 0.05.*

Reading a statement like this verifies the significance or lack of significance of the results by comparing the p level, the probability of the obtained statistic to the alpha level stated explicitly by the writer. In this case $p =0.016$, and is less than *alpha = 0.05*, therefore you can be 98.4 per cent certain the results were because of your design. It is customary to state the required significance level for statistical tests, which as we discussed before is conventionally set at 0.05. Also, note that in the APA format, statistics are generally reported to two decimal places, though p levels can be reported to three places for precision.

Common problems in data analysis

There are some common problems in data analysis. I have gathered them together into five categories:

- failing to fully consider data analysis at the planning stage;
- not fully organising and exploring data before carrying out data analysis;
- poor or wrong choice of statistical tests;
- poor or wrong decision making in evaluating the results of your data analyses;
- drawing of inappropriate, over-speculative or unsubstantiated conclusions.

Failing to fully consider data analysis at the planning stage

It is vital that the data analysis be as thought through in the planning stage as the methodology, the research question itself or the literature review. The data you wish to collect should help inform the design of the research project, so that should be taken one step further and consideration be given to the analysis method of that data. Too often I see research projects that grind to a halt because the data analysis was not considered at the planning stage. If it had been, the insurmountable hurdle that stopped it would in fact have been overcome.

Not fully organising and exploring data before carrying out data analysis

This was mentioned earlier in this chapter and it is important to do. It will identify, and therefore allow you to address, any potential problems early in the data collection. It is also important you begin to get a feel for trends and patterns that may emerge, so this exploration should not be rushed.

Poor or wrong choice of statistical tests

This is a frustrating problem that is often easily solved. Carrying out a research project for the first time is more about gaining experience of the process than really breaking new ground. Because of this, when it comes to the choice of statistical test, no one really expects you to know everything, therefore asking which one is best to use, and why, is the way forward. Supervisors and lecturers will be more than happy to advise you on this and so poor or wrong choices can be avoided.

Poor or wrong decision making in evaluating the results of your data analyses

As with the previous problem, this is a problem easily solved. Again your supervisor or lecturer will be glad to help. You must be able to correctly interpret and then evaluate the results of the tests you do.

Drawing of inappropriate, over-speculative or unsubstantiated conclusions

This is a potentially a serious problem that will undo a lot of hard work. I will cover it more in Chapter 12 when we look at how to write the discussion. Drawing of inappropriate, over-speculative or unsubstantiated conclusions shows either a lack of understanding or more seriously an intention to deceive, particularly when the conclusions are inappropriate or over-speculative. If anything researchers will often play down their findings, preferring to err on the side of caution. Science is evidence-based and so unsubstantiated conclusions are unacceptable.

Qualitative data analysis

So far this chapter has concentrated on the types of data analysis that would come from the collection of quantitative data. Research projects that follow a qualitative research paradigm are also very rich in data and need a very different type of analysis. I will set out and briefly describe a process below that will help start to achieve some examination of this rich form of data, but as with many things there is a lot more to analysing qualitative data and I have suggested further readings to help. The process is:

- organise the data;
- shape the data into information;
- interpret and summarise the information;
- explain the information.

Organise the data

Get the data into a format that is easy to work with. For example, notes from tape recordings will have to be transcribed. Written notes will have to be categorised and typed up. Video may have to be coded. After organising the data in this way, you should have an overall picture of the complete set of data.

Shape the data into information

After looking at the data, assess what type of themes are coming through. This analysis is done by sorting. Note down the different categories or types of responses found. You can use separate cards or sheets of paper to do this step, then start to separate the data into groups that share similar characteristics. Sticky notes and a large tabletop are useful here. Starting with a large number of categories will make it easier to allocate all the data. After becoming more familiar with the data and thinking about the relationships between the groups, it may be possible to reduce the number of categories.

Interpret and summarise the information

Do not try to quantify the responses, for example, you cannot say, *half the people said*, instead look for the range of views expressed. It is possible to say *some* or *others*, but you cannot say *most* or *few*. It is important to make sure all opinions or views are represented in the summary.

Explain the information

When trying to explain what the information means, it is advisable to discuss it at length with others. It is always better to be cautious about leaping to conclusions or making assumptions. The result of thinking about the information and relating it to what is already known will lead to an increase in knowledge and action.

Data analysis checklist

Use this checklist to prompt your thoughts on data analysis and also check with your supervisor how much interpretation you are required to include. Ask yourself:

- Have you used a structured approach for your analysis?
- Have you analysed the material in light of your research questions?
- Can you justify your analytical approach?
- Have you provided full details on the sample you used for your research?
- Have you used tables and graphs to good effect?
- Are you sure your graphs and tables show what you want them to?

Chapter Review

The take-home messages from this chapter are:

- Understand and explore your data from the very first data collection. There is very little time to waste in the progress of your project and the more time you can spend exploring and understanding the data you are actually collecting, the better it will make the conclusions you draw. You may start to see the patterns you expected, or you may start to see patterns you did not. Equally you may start to notice problems; if you have started to do this early, those problems can be rectified.

- Descriptive statistics and inferential statistics are used when your data is generally quantitative in nature. Qualitative data is generally very data rich but requires more care when using methods to analyse it.
- Gain a fuller understanding of statistical principles and methods in order to identify the correct tools to use in analysing your data. This fuller understanding will come from your own study of statistical texts, many of which are highlighted in the further reading that follows. Do not underestimate the help peers, learning support staff, supervisors and lecturers can give you in identifying, using and then interpreting the results from various statistical tests and statistical software packages.
- Three vital things to consider for your research project are: you should have absorbed some statistical thinking when designing your project; you understand the concept of probability; and you can test for significance if your data requires it.

Further Reading

There is a range of excellent sport and exercise texts that cover some statistical concepts and procedures. These texts have already been highlighted in earlier chapters. Another text that is very useful is:

- Williams, C (2004) *Data Analysis and Research for Sport and Exercise Science. A student guide.* London: Routledge.

Two further texts are excellent in gaining an understanding of quantitative statistical analyses and offer easy application to sport and exercise research projects. They are:

- Vincent, WJ (1999) *Statistics in Kinesiology.* Second edition. Champaign, IL: Human Kinetics.
- Salkind, NJ (2007) *Statistics for People Who (Think They) Hate Statistics.* London: Sage.

The British Medical Journal (BMJ) website contains good statistical papers and notes. The statistical notes by Bland and Altman are short and comprehensive papers on various statistical concepts but would be for a more advanced understanding of the topics.

Qualitative data analysis is also covered in the texts highlighted in the further reading of Chapter 6, *Non-experimental research*, but a very thought-provoking text about how qualitative data can be presented is:

- Sparkes, AC (2002) *Telling Tales in Sport and Physical Activity. A qualitative journey.* Champaign, IL: Human Kinetics.

Part 3
Crossing the finishing line

Chapter 11
Writing what you have found

Learning Objectives

This chapter will help you to be able to:

- understand the format and structure of your research report;
- understand the conventions of scientific writing;
- consider the likely audience of your research report and adjust your writing style to suit that audience.

You will also be able to:

- write an initial draft of your results.

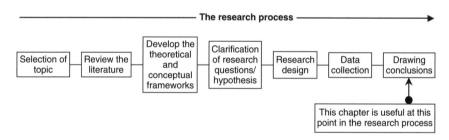

Figure 11.1 The research process: writing what you have found

Introduction

This chapter is essential for everyone who has to present a finished research project. Presenting your work is the culmination of your research project and to ensure that credit is given it is essential that the quality of that presentation reflects the quality of the research project itself. This chapter is the third of four chapters that break up the writing of your research project into manageable sections. By the end of each chapter you will be able to write first drafts of the sections that chapter covers.

- *Writing the why* covered the introduction and literature review.
- *Writing the how* covered the method.
- *Writing what you have found* covers the results.
- *Writing the so what* will cover the discussion and conclusion.

If you are presenting your research project in a different format to a conventional written report, such as a poster, there are still some important aspects that are common to scientific presentation, so it is still essential reading.

The accuracy and depth of analysis is often a distinguishing feature in deciding how good a research project is and therefore it is important that you identify an objective and structured way of considering your data and then presenting it. As your results show what you have achieved it is important that they are presented in the best light, as the way you set out your results will make a significant impact on the reader. Therefore it is worthwhile spending time not only thinking about what they mean but how to communicate this in the best way possible. Many readers will give up on your research if you present irrelevant material in a sloppy manner. Be clear about what you have found.

This chapter is essentially guidance on how to write the results from the data analysis that you have carried out. It links with Chapter 10, *Data analysis*, and at times you may want to refer to that chapter. In this chapter, how to write to make it count is discussed followed by a discussion on what you should choose to present. With those discussions in mind the remainder of the chapter goes on to look at how to present written results, tables and figures, with lots of guidance on the conventions to presenting this material. The checklist and summary at the end will then provide a further guide to ensure you are on track in your research report.

Write to make it count

The aim of the results section is to present your findings in a clear and unbiased way to the reader. Most results sections rely on tables and figures to do this but you also want to make it easy for the reader to understand the results of your research project. To help the reader of your work understand the results some text should accompany the inevitable tables and figures you provide. A reader of the results section should not have to try to figure out what is being shown, as it should be clear from the tables and figures and accompanied by relevant text. A way to check you are achieving this is to imagine that all the tables and graphs have been removed. Is the results section still comprehensible with just the text?

Whilst the majority of the results section will comprise tables and figures, the text accompanying those tables and figures should be clear and provide enough information for the reader to be able to figure out what is displayed. A mistake often seen is the cutting and pasting of tables and figures from the output of the statistical software package used with the original labels still shown. These labels, such as *var000001*, make no sense to the reader and so should be changed.

You may consider ending the results section with a brief summary of the key results if the research project was particularly complex, but remember any text used in the results section should be written to make it count.

Choose what to present

We know that the results should present your findings in a clear and unbiased way, but also you need to be selective about the findings you present. In Chapter 10 I pointed out that poor or wrong decision making in evaluating the results of your data analyses was a common mistake. Equally, it would be a mistake to present all your findings rather than selecting the most relevant. In the results section, less is often more. Just because there are three ways to show a measure of centrality in your data, that does not mean you should present them all, or just because you have analysed something for significance does not mean you have to present it. Where there are choices of different statistical techniques to demonstrate a certain concept choose the one most applicable and relevant, do not include them all; where you have analysed for significance present it if it is relevant to your research question.

A similar error is often found with the output from statistical software packages. There is usually a large amount of material produced in the outputs that sometimes include *post hoc* tests too. Not all of that output will be relevant or necessary to include in the results. From all the data you gather, process and analyse, you must be selective in what you choose to present. It is imperative that you consult with your supervisor or lecturer to seek advice as to what should and should not be included but go to them with a clear idea of how you think your results are relevant to your research question. Try to see the wood despite the trees.

Writing the results

When considering how to begin to write up the results you should consider some of the points made in Chapter 10, *Data analysis*, as they are closely related to your decisions here. This chapter is about how to present the results effectively once the analysis is done. Normally a report for a research project will contain the following sections in the results:

- a full description of the participant characteristics;
- a written description of the main findings;
- tables and figures of results.

It is important to note that throughout the results section no interpretation of what the results show should be attempted. The results are only discussed in the discussion. In this section it is important that the results are presented in an objective way. That also means that the style of language is in the third person and past tense as with the other sections of the research report.

Presenting the results in a logical sequence is also important. In the same way that the method was best presented in a chronological order, so too are the results. A reader can follow where the results have come from if they mirror the sequence in which they were presented in the method. In most research projects the first section presented would be the participant characteristics.

Participant characteristics

The participant characteristics are often the first thing in the results section and descriptive statistics are used to present that information. Usually the statistical description of the grouped participant characteristics is in the form of a table. The participants of your research project should be described as a group not as individuals, and so descriptive statistics will show the central tendency and the spread or variation of the group or groups that have participated. It is important to note here that, considering some of the issues that I highlighted in Chapter 8 (*You're off: making ethics applications*) about confidentiality, no participant should be able to be identified anywhere in the results section.

The purpose of describing the participant characteristics is so that the reader can assess the degree of homogeneity or heterogeneity of the group. If your research design used two or more groups, the characteristics of each group would normally be presented.

Written results

Usually any written analysis in the results section is the writing of the results of any inferential statistical tests that have been done. I highlighted in Chapter 10 how the reporting of the results of inferential statistical tests appears very simple but that there is a very specific format and style that should be followed when doing it.

The results only should be presented and so no discussion of what those results mean should take place. There is no discussion of critical values, null and alternative hypotheses, or of accepting or rejecting any hypothesis. Instead, the narrative should clearly indicate that the null hypothesis was either rejected or accepted and the alternative hypothesis was supported or not supported, simply by saying that the result was statistically significant or not. You may feel it necessary to state such things and your supervisor may also want you to if it is a first project, as this would help demonstrate understanding, but correct presentation of the results in written form can communicate this clearly.

The American Psychological Association (APA) produces a very detailed and specific set of guidelines on how to report the findings from inferential statistical tests; many institutions have adopted these as their own guidelines.

Tables and figures

The main findings of many studies are presented in tables and figures. A picture can say a thousand words but only when that picture is relevant to the thousand words you want to describe. When the word *figure* is used, it can often refer to a graph, a picture or a schematic but as normally only graphs are featured in the results section, *figure* will here refer to a graph. As the bulk of results sections are tables and figures, each one is examined in more detail.

Tables

Tables are very useful tools for summarising information into a concise and clear format. There are some specific conventions that should be followed when using tables in the results section. These are the:

- titling of tables;
- labelling within tables;
- format of tables.

When titling tables, the title should be such that the table can be understood without reference to the text. First attempts at titles can sometimes be quite wordy and so every effort must be made to be succinct with your writing. When you have initially titled a table, look for words that are superfluous and can be eliminated to ensure the title is as succinct as possible but still conveys all the information needed.

Labelling within tables is also important. Most tables require column headings and those headings should describe what is in that column and provide a unit of measurement in brackets if applicable. It is a common mistake in research reports by first-time researchers to forget to include units of measurement.

When considering the format of the table, you should think about the inclusion of horizontal and vertical lines and the alignment of the data within the table before it is drafted. Horizontal lines are used in tables to isolate the title of a column from the content of the column and to indicate the end of the table. You may also use horizontal lines to separate individual information from group information within the same table. Other than those reasons, horizontal lines are not needed in tables.

Vertical lines can also generally be avoided as long as the alignment of the data in the table is correct. Alignment of data can be to the left or right. If your data has values with decimal places, however, it is best aligned to the right as the decimal place will align and be consistent throughout the table as long as the number of decimals after the point is consistent. The usual number of places after the decimal is two. Table 11.1 is a good example of a table produced for a research report.

Group	Age (yr)	Weight (kg)	VO_2 max (ml/min/kg)
Group 1	25 ± 4.9	72 ± 3.6	55 ± 3.1
Group 2	26 ± 3.4	71 ± 3.4	52 ± 2.4

Table 11.1: An example of a table produced for a research report.
Characteristics of participants, Mean $\pm$ SD

Learning Activity 11.1

Now you have guidance on how to draft a table, use the information about your participants to draft a table of the participant characteristics for the participants of your research project. You may have to refer to an earlier section of this chapter, 'Participant characteristics', and to Chapter 10 to understand what should be in that table and how to present descriptive statistics.

Figures

Figures, or specifically graphs, are also very useful tools for summarising information into a concise and clear format that a reader can easily understand at a glance. As with tables there are some specific conventions that should be followed when using graphs. These are:

- using the correct graph for the information you wish to present;
- titling of graphs;
- labelling within graphs;
- format of graphs.

Graphs are used when the information you wish to present is:

- plotted in relation to a continuous variable, such as time;
- of two more groups that you wish to compare.

Graphs can be used to present other information and that is also discussed here. When presenting data that is plotted in relation to a continuous variable, such as time, a line graph is suitable. A note of caution with line graphs is that points of a line graph should only be joined if the points are related in some way. It is a common mistake to try to join points that should not be joined. It is also important to choose the correct variables for the x and y axes. As a guide the independent variable forms the x-axis and the dependent variable forms the y-axis. An example of a typical line graph from a research report is shown in Figure 11.2.

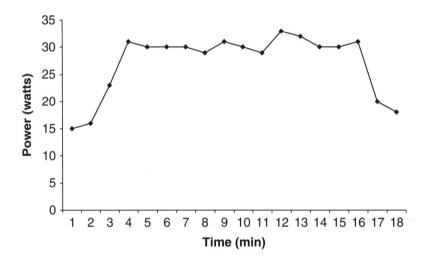

Figure 11.2 Example of a line graph from a research report. Power output over time.

If the points on the graph just refer to individual participants and are not related then a scatter plot would be the best graph to use in that case.

When comparing the data of two or more groups, a bar chart, sometimes known as a histogram, is used. Bar charts do not differ significantly from column charts. Bar charts can also be used when the same measurement is made on several occasions in a group of participants. An example of a bar chart from a research report is shown in Figure 11.3.

Another graph often seen in research reports is a pie chart. A pie chart is useful when your data falls into categories.

As with tables, when titling graphs the title should be such that the table can be understood without reference to the text. The normal convention for the placing of the title of a graph is to place it either at the side or underneath the graph it refers to.

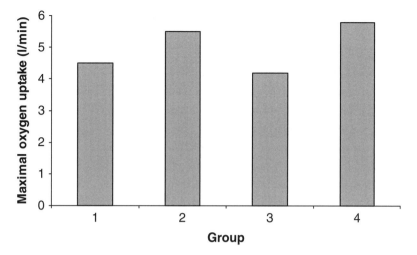

Figure 11.3 Example of a bar chart from a research report. Maximal oxygen uptake (l/min).

Labelling, particularly of the axes, within figures is important. The axis label should describe what is shown on that axis and provide a unit of measurement in brackets.

The format of the graph should convey the data in a clear way. It is sometimes tempting to use some of the more exotic designs that software packages can use, but this should be avoided.

Writing-up checklist

You can find this checklist, which we first used in Chapter 9, in the Appendix.

Chapter Review

The take-home messages from this chapter are:

- You should not present all of the material you have that constitutes results from your data analysis. You are writing to communicate your findings in a clear, concise, unbiased way and so you should be selective about what you choose to present and how best to present that material.
- The written presentation of results, along with tables and figures, has a very specific convention that should be followed. Many readers will give up on your research if you present irrelevant material in a sloppy manner, so ensure that you understand and follow these conventions.
- It is essential that the results section of your report links to all the other sections. Consider your research question when considering the results to present, consider the sequence of your method when considering the sequence in presenting your results. Have thoughts about what the analysis means and how that compares to your original thoughts but do not present that information in this section. That is for the discussion.

Further Reading

In previous chapters I have highlighted many key texts that are specific to sport and exercise and that I consider excellent relevant help to that particular chapter. Most of these texts will have useful guidance on how to write an introduction, literature review or results section. For the results section it is highly recommended you seek the website or guidance of the American Psychological Association (APA) as many institutions will use the APA guidelines as their own.

For these chapters on writing I suggest a range of books that provide excellent help for writing in general. These include both texts for writing specifically and texts for study skills that will include help for writing. For a list of these titles, please see the 'Further Reading' section at the end of Chapter 7.

Chapter 12
Writing the so what

This chapter will help you to be able to:

- understand the format and structure of your research report;
- understand the conventions of scientific writing;
- consider the likely audience of your research report and adjust your writing style to suit that audience.

You will also be able to:

- write an initial draft of your discussion and conclusions.

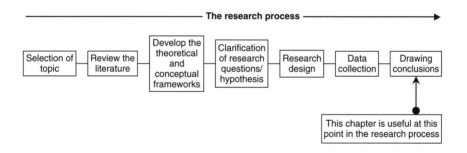

Figure 12.1 The research process: writing the so what

Introduction

This chapter is essential for everyone who has to present a finished research project. Presenting your work is the culmination of your research project and to ensure that credit is given it is essential that the quality of that presentation reflects the quality of the research project itself. This chapter is the fourth of four chapters that break up the writing of your research project into manageable sections. By the end of each chapter you will be able to write first drafts of the sections that chapter covers.

- *Writing the why* covered the introduction and literature review.
- *Writing the how* covered the method.

- *Writing what you have found* covered the results.
- *Writing the so what* covers the discussion and conclusion.

If you are presenting your research project in a different format to a conventional written report, such as a poster, there are still some important aspects that are common to scientific presentation, so it is still essential reading.

This chapter is about how to discuss the results that you have, in relation both to your research questions and the existing knowledge in and around the topic area of your research. This is your opportunity to highlight how your research project and its findings reflect, differ from and extend the current knowledge of the area in which you have chosen to carry out research. This chapter is your chance to demonstrate exactly what you know about this topic by interpreting your findings and outlining what they mean. It brings the whole project to a close and closes the circle of research that I highlighted in Chapter 7. At the end of your discussion you should have examined and considered all of the results that you found and provided an explanation for your findings.

It is important that this section is comprehensive and structured. Links back to the literature you reviewed earlier in the project should be made clear. The discussion offers the opportunity to demonstrate the value of your research and it is therefore very important to discuss your work thoroughly.

This chapter will examine how to write to make it count, and how to write a strong discussion. It then looks at each particular suggested subsection, moving from the specific summary of your research to the general theoretical and/or practical implications of your findings. Finally some checklists will help ensure you are on your way to completing an excellent research project.

Write to make it count

The discussion section is probably the least formalised part of the report as there needs to be the flexibility in the structure to allow every type of research project to be discussed. In simple terms the aim of the discussion is to tell the reader what to make of the results you have obtained. If you have written the results section well the reader should already recognise the trends in the data and have an emerging idea of whether your research question has been answered or your hypothesis supported if you have one. Because the results can seem so self-explanatory you may find it tough to know what material to add in this last section. It is very self-satisfying but not very professional to simply write in the discussion, *I told you so*. Conversely you may be thinking, *How could I have got it wrong?*, if the results indicate the opposite to your original thinking. Either viewpoint requires you to now examine the evidence and to interpret the research. The key to a good discussion is a clear understanding of what the research means. This can only be done if the results are interpreted correctly. You also need to discuss your research coherently. A good discussion presents a coherent, well-structured explanation that accounts for the findings of the research, making links between the evidence obtained and existing knowledge, regardless of whether you are in a *I told you so* or *how could I have got it wrong* position.

Reflection Point

Sarah completed a research project in sport and exercise and her findings did not match her original thoughts when she started the process. She was in a *how could I have got it wrong* position. I remember clearly her comments when I discussed with her how she found the process.

I started to think as I began to analyse my results that things were not turning out as I had thought they would. The more this became clear, the more I worried. Honestly, I started to panic a little. A friend helped me and I realised that I had to go back and re-examine where I had developed my original ideas. As soon as I did that I started to see where the links were between what I had done and importantly not done. Because of this I had a lot to discuss and it was brilliant.

The point Sarah highlights here is that the results of research are neither right nor wrong, they are just the outcomes from a process. How you then discuss that process in terms of how you:

- explain whether the data support your original thinking;
- acknowledge any anomalous data or deviations from what you expected;
- derive conclusions, based on your findings;
- relate findings to earlier work; and
- explore the theoretical and/or practical implications of your findings

determines what makes a strong discussion.

How to write a strong discussion section

Writing a strong discussion is essential to demonstrate the value of your work. A comprehensive and well-structured discussion that makes clear links back to the literature you reviewed earlier in the research project is the culmination of the whole process. To write a strong discussion, you need to be able to structure an argument coherently, provide evidence for that argument and yet still remain objective. The links between how to write this section and writing the literature review are clear and so a review of Chapter 4 and your literature review would be a step towards writing a strong discussion.

To create a logical and coherent structure to the discussion you should consider breaking the whole into several parts. The order of these parts can be varied slightly but generally the reverse of the structure of how you presented material in your introduction and literature review works best. That is, you should move from the specific, related to your research project only, to the general, how your findings fit in the larger research community. These parts should include:

- a summary of your findings;
- relationship of your findings to previous research;
- discussion of the limitations of your research project;
- acknowledgement of anomalous data or deviations from what you expected;

- exploration of the theoretical and/or practical implications of your findings;
- suggestions for further research;
- conclusions and recommendations.

Writing the discussion

A discussion is not simply a summary of the results you have. It is important at this stage that you demonstrate original thinking. This can be a two-stage process. First, you should highlight and discuss how your research has reinforced what is already known about the area. Many undertaking a research project for the first time make the mistake of thinking that they should have found something new. The reality is there are very few research projects that have findings that are completely unique. Instead, you are likely to have a number of findings that reinforce what is already known about the field and you need to highlight these, explaining why you think this has occurred.

Second, you may have discovered something different or that does not seem to fit nicely into what is already known about the field. You should outline what is new and how this compares to what is already known. You should also attempt to provide an explanation as to why your research identified these differences. From this you can then consider how your results extends the knowledge in the field. Even if you found similarities between your results and the existing work of others, your research extends knowledge of the area, by reinforcing current thinking. You should state how it does this, as this is a legitimate finding. If it contrasts to what is already known about the field, the *why* to why it contrasts is important to discuss and explore.

Summarise your findings

A discussion should begin with a brief summary of the principal results of your research project. The principal results should be concise and clear. Consider the reader of your work, they may have skipped the results section completely or they may need it refreshed in their minds. Be careful not to include statistics or excessive detail though, if the reader wanted that they could read the results again!

A hypothesis and the summary

If your research project has a hypothesis a good way to begin the discussion is to state how the results support or do not support your hypothesis. After all, you cannot really discuss the larger scientific value of your study until you have explained to the reader if the particulars of the experiment have provided evidence to do this or not. You might begin the discussion by explicitly stating the differences, relationships or correlations your data indicate between the independent and dependent variables. Then you can show more clearly why you believe your hypothesis was or was not supported later. For example, if you tested the effect of caffeine on reaction times at various times in training you could start this section by noting that the effect of caffeine on reaction time increased as the time spent training increased and therefore supported the hypothesis. If your initial hypothesis surmised that caffeine would have no effect on reaction times at various times in training, you would then say something like, the hypothesis that caffeine would have an effect on reaction times at various times in training was not supported by the data.

Do not worry about providing too much information. Remember the discussion is there to provide a logical, coherently structured argument and the summary provides the taster of what is to come.

Also, recognise that saying whether the data supported your hypothesis or not involves making a claim to be defended. As such, you need to show the readers that this claim is supported by the evidence. Make sure that you are very explicit about the relationship between the evidence and the conclusions you draw from it. This process is difficult for many writers because we do not often justify conclusions in our everyday lives. In a scientific research report you need to defend any claim thoroughly.

Reflection Point

So far I have not highlighted any conventions that should be followed in writing the discussion. That is because the conventions of other sections still stand in that the writing should be in the third person and the past tense. However, whilst strictly not a convention of writing, some examination of the language used in the discussion is worthwhile.

A common mistake in discussions is that any conclusions drawn can be inappropriate, over-speculative or unsubstantiated. This particular mistake is discussed later in this chapter but something that contributes to this is the language used by the writer when drawing conclusions. Words such as *know*, or *true*, or *confirmed* could infer to a reader that your single research project has provided definitive evidence. Researchers tend to be very circumspect when drawing conclusions and are unlikely to claim that what has been found in one study allows a claim that something is now *known*, or *true*, or *confirmed*. In your writing hesitate before you claim such things; less absolutely conclusive language, including such words as *suggest*, *indicate*, *correspond*, *possibly*, *challenge*, etc. is much better.

When referring to the hypothesis the same is true. Earlier I used the terminology of *support* or *not support* when referring to the hypothesis. A common mistake is that you say the hypothesis was *proved* or *disproved* or that it was *correct* or *incorrect*. These terms, however, reflect a degree of certainty that you as a researcher are not supposed to have if you are to provide an objective view. Remember, you are testing a theory with a procedure that is very likely to have many flaws and drawbacks and this would severely compromise your ability to be sure about the *truth* you see. Words like *supported*, *indicated*, and *suggested* are more acceptable ways to evaluate your hypothesis. In time, and with further evidence, you may be able to use more definitive words, particularly if you make the topic your lifetime study!

Relate your findings to previous research

Throughout this research project you have been working as a researcher in sport and exercise and as such you, by default, belong to a community of fellow researchers. The aim has been in each section of the research report to write within conventions recognised and accepted by the research community to which you belong. The discussion section of the report, in part, is exactly that, a discussion. Therefore part of this process and an aim of this particular section is to try to identify a conversation going on among members of your research community, and use your work to contribute to that conversation. Identifying the conversation was actually achieved very early in the research project. It was when you researched the literature of your community to discover the questions that were worthy of investigation. Now you are contributing your thoughts, backed by evidence, back to that community.

Relating your findings to previous research requires some consideration. An understanding of the context is vital to the reader to be able to see the relationships you see. When writing your introduction you attempted to put the research project into context. This was so the reader could fully understand the value of your research. You gave a sense of the context that provoked and nourished the research project. You need to do this again and to recognise what is new about your research project and its findings and how it benefits the wider body of scientific knowledge. On a more pragmatic level, especially for first-time researchers who may be producing the research for an academic project, connecting your work to previous research will demonstrate that you see the big picture. You have an opportunity in the discussion section to distinguish yourself from others who may not think beyond the barest facts. Capitalise on this opportunity by putting your own work in context.

From the context you can then make the links to previous research. If you are a first-time researcher most likely the work you have done has already been performed and you could probably point to a similar project or study and compare/contrast your results and conclusions. More advanced work may deal with an issue that is somewhat less resolved, and so previous research may take the form of an ongoing debate, and you can use your own work to contribute to that debate. Consider that you have probably already written material you can adapt in the introduction about this debate as background.

Now that you have findings, the background and findings of previous research you presented in the introduction can be compared and contrasted to your own work. It may require some specific information about your study when you attempt to explain your observations. Allow some creative thinking to be presented here – not too much of course – but this part offers an opportunity for you to show your flair for understanding previous research and your own findings and being able to fit it all together into a coherent argument.

Discuss the limitations of your research project

In an ideal world the research project you have carried out is ideal and has no limitations. Sadly, it is not an ideal world and as with all research projects there have been limitations to your work. These limitations may have been external or internal; either way they will have influenced the results and are worthy of discussion.

Discussing the limitations of your research project should not be the part where you beat yourself up, neither should it be the part where you can lay blame or fault for all that went wrong. Instead it should be reflective and an opportunity to communicate to others the lessons you have learned from the research project.

Look for the methodological problems that have affected your findings: was the dose you used too small to produce an effect? Should you have left your participants longer in the ice bath? Be careful here not to suggest obvious limitations to which the response from your reader could be, *Well, why didn't you then?* An example of this is the common statement, *The research would have benefited from more participants.* Statements like this are obvious and do not demonstrate evaluation of your research project to any depth.

This part of the discussion provides a chance to pre-empt any of the reader's criticisms before they can offer them. State clearly what your limitations have been, but equally discuss why or how they were compensated for. It is likely some of the limitations will play an important part in the conclusions you draw from your findings.

Acknowledging anomalous data or deviations from what you expected

Part of collecting data for any research project is the fact that you are likely to gather anomalous data or deviations from what you expected. You need to take these exceptions and divergences into account so that you qualify your conclusions sufficiently. For obvious reasons, your readers will doubt your authority if you deliberately or inadvertently overlook a key piece of data that does not quite match with your perspective on what occurred. In a more philosophical sense, once you have ignored evidence that contradicts your claims, you have departed from the experimental or scientific method that I discussed in Chapter 5. The urge to *tidy up* data is often strong, but if you give in to it you are no longer performing good research.

Acknowledging anomalous data or deviations from what you expected is part of discussing the limitations of your research project. Often after you have performed a data collection you realise that some part of the method you used was flawed. This may be the reason why you have deviations from what you expected. In this case it is fine to suggest that if you had the chance to repeat the research project again, you might change the design in this or that specific way in order to avoid such problems. The key to making this approach work, though, is to be very precise about the weakness in your research project, why and how you think that weakness might have affected your data, and how you would alter your protocol to eliminate or limit the effects of that weakness.

Anomalous data can be a little trickier to explain. In some cases it may be just an error in how it was recorded, and if that is the case it should have been excluded. It may be that it is a *freak* result. Often, inexperienced researchers feel the need to account for anomalous data and speculate about what might have caused such a result. If you have such a result, make an informed decision about whether to include that data or not. To exclude is often better than offering poor excuses for anomalous results that do not indicate that the research project had weaknesses.

Explore the theoretical and/or practical implications of your findings

Remember earlier I said that the discussion should move in its structure from the specifics of your research project to the general, and exploring the theoretical and/or practical implications of your findings brings the discussion to a logical general end. For research work in sport and exercise, or in any subject for that matter, to have importance, it should have clear theoretical and/or practical implications. This ties up the thoughts of *so what* that were explored in the introduction. The theoretical and/or practical implications of your research project are the tangible *so whats*.

As the discussion should be a logical coherent argument you want to use words that convey the main point of your writing. This main point can be primarily theoretical, *Understanding of this area gives a greater understanding of the larger topic area of . . .*, or primarily practical, *This information can be used to take such and such an action in terms of. . . .* In either case, the concluding statements help the reader to comprehend the significance of your project and your decision to write about it.

Make suggestions for further research

Any research project should leave a number of openings for further research. It should not be more questions unanswered than answered but instead new questions posed. It is exciting to feel that your research project is perhaps just the beginning of many more to come.

A common mistake in writing this part of the discussion is to simply be glib, by suggesting further research that is a variation of the research that has already been done without any clear rationale for doing that. Any suggestions for further research should have a clear brief explanation of why it would be worth doing and what it might show.

Draw some conclusions and recommendations

This part of the discussion pulls together the analysis and discussion of your research project in order to say what your research actually means. The conclusion of your research should provide a final critical reflection on your research project and its contribution to literature and the area of investigation. It should also point to issues that could be pursued in future research. It comes from the answers to the *so what* question that fellow researchers will use to evaluate your work and gives you the opportunity to demonstrate that you know what your research means.

Conclusions are usually short and should not contain new material. They are often difficult to write as you are likely to feel that you have said it all by this stage. As a result, many researchers simply summarise what they have said previously; unfortunately, this is not concluding. Concluding is giving the take-home message to your reader.

The conclusion of your research has three main roles. First, it provides an ending to the project. It provides the opportunity for you to say what your research means. Second, it provides you with the opportunity to say how your research can contribute to the understanding of the knowledge in the area of sport and exercise you have researched. Third, it leaves the reader with a final impression of the quality of your work.

It is very important to take the time to make conclusions about your work. By this stage of your research project, your enthusiasm for your research may be waning. It is likely you are trying to write this section under the pressure of deadlines. Researchers and those who assess your work want to see sensible conclusions being made from research as this demonstrates that the researcher has fully understood what they have done. As this part of your project pretty much stands on its own, make sure that you are clear about what is required from a conclusion. This will make the process much easier.

Drawing of inappropriate, over-speculative or unsubstantiated conclusions

I mentioned this briefly earlier in this chapter, and in particular how the language you use in the discussion can give the perception that you are drawing inappropriate, over-speculative or unsubstantiated conclusions. To do this is potentially damaging and can undo a lot of your hard work. Drawing inappropriate, over-speculative or unsubstantiated conclusions shows either a lack of understanding or more seriously an intention to deceive. If anything researchers often will play down their findings, preferring to err on the side of caution. Be cautious in drawing your conclusions. Draw only conclusions you can substantiate with evidence. Limit your conclusions to the scope of your research project and not outside its boundaries. Use language that is circumspect rather than definitive.

Discussion checklist

This checklist will be useful in checking you are meeting the typical requirements for the discussion. However, ensure you check with your supervisor or lecturers as to your institution's specific requirements.

- Do you know what form your discussion section can/must take?
- Is there a word limit? What is it?
- Will your supervisor read a draft?
- Is there work from previous research you can look at? Were they assessed by the same criteria as you?
- Have you provided a brief summary of your results at the start of the section to remind the reader what you have found?
- Have you explained the key findings of your research?
- Have you placed your results in the context of existing knowledge by comparing your findings with the existing literature?
- Have you considered your findings in the light of your research questions?
- Have you provided a convincing explanation of your research?
- Have you proofread your work?
- Have you included full reference details in a consistent and approved form?

Writing-up checklist

You can find this checklist, which we first used in Chapter 9, in the Appendix.

Chapter Review

The take-home messages from this chapter are:

- The discussion is a logically sequenced coherent argument that represents the culmination of your work. It requires planning and drafting to do well and should link clearly to the previous work included in the introduction and literature review. Spend some considerable time reviewing and redrafting your work in the discussion, literature review and introduction.

- The discussion should be ordered in a sequence from the specifics of your research to the general and should include a summary of your findings, some discussion of the limitations of your research project, acknowledgement of any anomalous data or deviations from what you expected, an exploration of the theoretical and/or practical implications of your findings, some suggestions for further research, and conclusions. In each of these sections you should attempt to say what your research means. Say how the research contributes to knowledge about the area by making final links to literature, theoretical understanding and practice.
- Be aware that the language you use in the discussion sets the tone to the reader on how sure you are about the findings of your research. It is always best to be circumspect regarding claims that you make, as to err on the side of caution is a better place to be when more experienced and possibly knowledgeable readers will be assessing your work.

Further Reading

In previous chapters I have highlighted many key texts that are specific to sport and exercise and that I consider excellent relevant help to that particular chapter. Most of those texts will have useful guidance on how to write a discussion.

For these chapters on writing I suggest a range of books that provide excellent help for writing in general. These include both texts for writing specifically and texts for study skills that will include help for writing. For a list of these titles, please see the 'Further Reading' section at the end of Chapter 7.

Chapter 13
Crossing the finishing line

From the instant you picked up this text and began to prepare to carry out a research report in sport and exercise you have been working towards this moment. This is crossing the finishing line, the final handing in of a lot of hard work, blood, sweat and tears. Well done. If you can keep the momentum going for just a little longer you can complete the task, sit back and relax. Once the research report has been submitted there is very little else you can do.

Learning Objectives

This chapter will help you to be able to:

- write an effective title and abstract for your report;
- consider the citing and referencing of the work of others that you have used;
- seek appropriate guidance on the specifics of writing English in a report format.

You will also be able to:

- complete the research report.

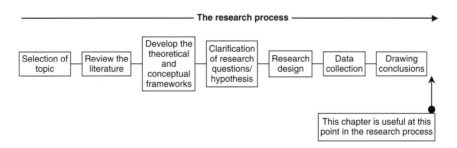

Figure 13.1 The research process: crossing the finishing line

Introduction

Now you need to pull your research together into a well-presented, cohesive report. This text takes you through the entire process of writing up the report and you will have already absorbed what it has had to say; however, now is the time to return to these chapters and read them in more detail. When you have done this, you should be clear about what has to be done to achieve the final written report.

As with the other chapters that you have read about writing your research report, this chapter is essential for everyone who has to present that research project in some format. Presenting your work is the culmination of your research project and to ensure that credit is given it is essential that the quality of that presentation reflects the quality of the research project itself. Previous chapters about writing have concentrated on writing the bulk of the content of that report. This chapter is more concerned with general issues of presentation and the smaller, final finishes a quality research report requires.

This chapter is really about adding the finishing touches to a lot of hard work. Finishing touches include vital aspects such as adding an effective title to your work, writing the abstract and ensuring you are referencing correctly. The further reading gives direction to a number of texts you can use to help support your writing.

The title of your report

The title of a research report is the thing that will catch the attention of a potential reader. They may have searched for literature as you did, scanned the list of articles and those with titles of interest would be read. So the title of your report needs to give the reader an idea of what the research report is about while still remaining snappy and to the point.

It is not important to think about the title until your report is nearly finished, although you may have been using a working title for your research until now. It is normally a minor point when compared to the whole project, but now is the time to get it right.

An effective title should be clear and specific and should not be vague or too long and convoluted. To prevent your title becoming too wordy, look for the superfluous words that can be eliminated. I often see titles for first-time research projects that begin *A study of* . . . and I immediately think, there are three words that could be eliminated! A good tip for writing a title for those who have used an experimental research design is to include the independent and dependent variables in your title.

The abstract

The abstract is usually the next thing to be read after the title and its purpose is to summarise the whole research report in a short, clear form. As it summarises the report as a whole it is the first thing to be read but yet the last to actually be written.

I personally find writing an abstract a very difficult thing to do. This is because you are attempting to summarise 7,000 or 10,000 words into something as short as 120 or 150 words. That is not an easy task.

Because an abstract is very short and it should give the reader an overview of the whole of the research project, you need to avoid excessive amounts of detail and keep it simple, clear and to the point. Aim to write one or two sentences that describe the key elements of your research, beginning with the rationale for the project, through the methods used, the results and finally the principal conclusions you have made.

Referencing

The referencing of work that has been included is often something first-time researchers find difficult to manage effectively. It is easy to make mistakes when referencing the work of others in your own work, but it is very important not to make any. This is because the whole purpose of referencing and the reference section is to allow the reader of your work to gain access to the works you have used in your report.

The method for referencing and how the reference section should be presented is normally specified by your institution. A very common method in use is the Harvard system.

The Harvard system suggests that when you cite within the text of your report, that is when you show you have used the work of another in the text; the citation should normally include the author's surname and the year of publication. This information then allows the reader to consult the reference section at the end of the report to get full details of the actual work used. The process of citing and referencing sounds relatively simple, but I know from my own personal experience that the number of and different types of work that I cite and then reference gives all sorts of variety to how it should be written accurately and correctly in the text and reference section. For example, consider how all the different types of sources of work the internet can provide need to be referenced.

Rather than give details of how to reference every possible source that you may have used I would refer you first to your institution. Your institution will normally specify the style of referencing that should be used. This is normally supported by guidance from lecturing staff, your supervisor or learning centre staff. Second, the further reading of this chapter will give a guide for useful texts to consult for further guidance on referencing.

Write to make it count

Throughout the chapters on writing I have emphasised that your writing should be such that you write to make it count. Writing to make it count is about transferring the research that you have done into a well-structured and well presented research report.

I assume that this is particularly important to most readers of this text as the research report is likely to be presented as an assessed piece of work submitted to an academic institution as part of an award. Most research projects are assessed primarily, if not solely, by the research report or dissertation. It is therefore important that your research report communicates what you have done, why you have done it and what you have found. In order to do your research justice and to get a good mark, it is essential that you produce an integrated and cohesive report that documents your research in a concise and objective manner. It will also need to be well presented as most examiners are put off by a poorly laid out and badly proofread document.

To write to make it count and to make your research count, you need to bear two things in mind.

First, your report needs to present your research accurately, usually starting with the research objectives and the literature review and finishing with conclusions about your results in terms of these objectives and the existing literature. This *vertical thread* that runs throughout your project report will ensure that your research is presented as an integrated whole. Also it should not draw any inappropriate, over-speculative or unsubstantiated conclusions.

Second, does it look good? You may think that this is a secondary issue but not only is a well-presented report easier to read, it also communicates the essence of your research findings more effectively. Poorly structured, badly organised reports make it harder for the reader to work out the message that you are actually trying to get over; they obscure and therefore diminish the impact of your findings. Producing well-presented work also demonstrates that you have been able to manage the research process sufficiently well to ensure that you have time to take care over the presentation of the end result.

As the mark that you will be awarded is likely to be contingent on these two factors, it is critical to be concerned with both content and presentation.

Crossing the finishing line checklist

This final checklist is a useful aide-mémoire to ensure you have achieved what you set out to do from the beginning of the research project to its completion. Use it to help you ensure all is done that needs to be.

- In what form must the research be presented?
- What are the conventions, such as the layout and the referencing style that your institution requires you to follow?
- Are you within the word limit?
- When do you have to submit your report?
- Do you have to get your project bound? If so, how long will this take?
- How many copies do you have to submit?
- How will this piece of work be assessed? What are the criteria?
- Is there work from previous students you can look at? Were they assessed by the same criteria as you?
- Have you any final questions for your supervisor?
- Have you expressed the objectives of your research in a clear manner?
- Have you presented a relevant and up-to-date literature review?
- Did you carry out your research in a valid and reliable manner?
- Have you explained what method you used in enough detail to allow others to repeat your research?
- Have you reported the findings of your research in an objective manner?
- Is there a clear explanation of how the findings of your research relate to what we already know about the topic?
- What does your research mean? What conclusions can be drawn from it?
- Does your project contain a *vertical thread*?
- Have you structured your arguments well?
- Have you proofread your report? Have you got someone else to proofread your report?
- Have you included full reference details in a consistent and approved format?
- Have you laid it out clearly?
- Are you sure you haven't plagiarised any work?

Is it too late?

Write! By now you will have completed your research and as a result have knowledge that should be shared. It can sometimes be quite daunting to try and convert the mass of data that you have obtained into a logical, concise report. You will hopefully be at a point when most of the work is complete and the required sections are written. What if you are not in this position? If that is the case, start to write now. One of the major problems that students face when carrying out research is underestimating how difficult it is, and how long it takes to write up research. If you do not know how to start, begin with the method section as this simply requires you to outline what you did for your research. This will get you into the process of writing and it should become easier from there.

Chapter Review

The take-home messages from this chapter are:

- The title needs to be concise, clear and attractive to a potential reader. It should not be ambiguous or vague.
- The abstract of your research report requires the project to be complete and written before you can write it. Again, it needs to be concise yet detailed enough that it conveys all the necessary detail for a reader to make a judgement as to whether the work is worthy of further reading.
- Referencing is a key part of any research report and great care should be taken to ensure you cite and reference correctly and accurately, adhering to the preferred referencing style of your institution.
- It is never too late. Taking one step towards completing something ensures it is one step closer to being complete.

Further Reading

This text is not the only support you should seek. As I outlined earlier in this text, lecturers, supervisors and learning centre staff, amongst others, are all resources you should draw upon. Guidance as to how to write, rather than what to write, is sometimes also necessary. The resources identified below are further reading suggestions to help you with your writing. They cover the key elements which contribute to producing a good research report that include:

- producing a complete report, covering the main areas expected of a research project and writing in a manner that ensures that it all fits together;
- writing in an objective, coherent and grammatically correct manner;
- technical skills, such as referencing and acknowledging other people's work.

These resources will in addition guide you on aspects of writing, such as constructing sentences, paragraphs, using punctuation and grammar. Some are very lengthy and contain conventions that may not be relevant to your work, for example American spelling of words, but are still useful. They will also include guidance on editing and proofreading, formatting and referencing. Be careful not to spend too much time reading the technical information on how to write. Once you have started to write, you can go back to these sources if you need further clarification.

You need to use these resources purposefully, to help you perform to your best in meeting the specific requirements of your own institution. As ever, that should be your starting point. For example, at your particular institution, do you have to include an acknowledgements section or full transcripts of interviews? What typeface, line spacing and page numbering is required? Find out, and then use the resources accordingly.

Skim the contents of these resources if they are available to you and select those sources which are most relevant to your requirements. You will have come across this material already if you have accessed it from further reading in other chapters. You may prefer to rely mainly on one source, but it is usually helpful to read a few.

- Pritchard, A (2008) *Studying and Learning at University. Vital skills for success in your degree.* London: Sage.
- Barrass, R (2002) *Scientists Must Write.* Second edition. London: Routledge.
- Burns, T and Sinfield, S (2008) *Essential Study Skills. The complete guide to success at university.* Second edition. London: Sage.
- Turk, C (2001) *Effective Writing. Improving scientific, technical and business communication.* Second edition. London: Spon Press.
- Johnson, W (2007) *Write to the Top.* New York: Palgrave Macmillan.
- O'Connor, M (1999) *Writing Successfully in Science.* London: E & F N Spon.

Appendix: writing-up checklist

- Have you set yourself deadlines and kept to them?
- Do you write regularly?
- When you have completed your reading for one section do you write it up?
- Do you check that you have covered all essential requirements of the section of the report you are working on?
- Are you taking care to stay within the required word limit and your targeted limit for that section?
- Ensure that you keep the structure of your report simple and easy to follow; use sub-headings to help structure individual sections.
- Think carefully about how you will ensure that the core chapters – i.e. *Literature review*, *Research methodology*, *Results* and *Analysis and discussion* – link together. The use of sub-headings that relate to each other may help you to avoid the trap of losing the focus of your research.
- Number tables and figures and provide titles.
- Check your referencing system is correct. Make sure you have acknowledged your sources.
- Check your bibliography for errors.
- Give yourself time to revise your writing and ask someone to proofread it for mistakes in grammar, paragraph structure, spelling and understanding.
- Avoid using jargon and technical language as much as possible. Where this is used, explain its meaning to the reader.
- Check that you have stated the aims of the research clearly.
- Remember to see your supervisor regularly for help and guidance.
- *Do not* give up – most people find it difficult to write, even those who write for a living.

References

Andrews, D (2005) *Qualitative Methods in Sports Studies*. New York: Berg.

Barrass, R (2002) *Scientists Must Write*. Second edition. London: Routledge.

Berg, K (2004) *Essentials of Research Methods in Health, Physical Education, Exercise Science and Recreation*. Second edition. Baltimore: Lippincott Williams and Wilkins.

Bernard, C (1949) *An Introduction to the Study of Experimental Medicine*. Henry Schuman.

Burns, T and Sinfield, S (2008) *Essential Study Skills. The complete guide to success at university*. Second edition. London: Sage.

Davies, MB (2007) *Doing a Successful Research Project*. Basingstoke: Palgrave Macmillan.

Field, A (2003) *How to Design and Report Experiments*. London: Sage.

Gratton, C and Jones, I (2003) *Research Methods for Sport Studies*. London: Routledge.

Grix, J (2004) *The Foundations of Research*. Basingstoke: Palgrave Macmillan.

Johnson, W (2007) *Write to the Top*. New York: Palgrave Macmillan.

Long, J (2007) *Researching Leisure, Sport and Tourism. The essential guide*. London: Sage.

McNamee, M (2006) *Research Ethics in Exercise, Health and Sports Sciences*. Abingdon: Routledge.

O'Connor, M (1999) *Writing Successfully in Science*. London: E & F N Spon.

Pritchard, A (2008) *Studying and Learning at University. Vital skills for success in your degree*. London: Sage.

Rummel, JF (1963) *Research Methodology in Business*. New York: Harper & Row.

Salkind, NJ (2007) *Statistics for People Who (Think They) Hate Statistics*. London: Sage.

Sparkes, AC (2002) *Telling Tales in Sport and Physical Activity. A qualitative journey*. Champaign, IL: Human Kinetics.

Tenenbaum, G (2005) *Methods of Research in Sport Sciences. Quantitative and qualitative approaches*. Oxford: Meyer and Meyer Sport.

Thomas, J (1996) *Research Methods in Physical Activity*. Third edition. Champaign, IL: Human Kinetics.

Turk, C (2001) *Effective Writing. Improving scientific, technical and business communication*. Second Edition. London: Spon Press.

Vincent, WJ (1999) *Statistics in Kinesiology*. Second edition. Champaign, IL: Human Kinetics.

Williams, C (2004) *Data Analysis and Research for Sport and Exercise Science. A student guide*. London: Routledge.

Index